Management Buy-Out

Management Buy-Out

A guide for the prospective entrepreneur

Ian Webb

Gower

Published by
Gower Publishing Company Limited,
Gower House,
Croft Road,
Aldershot,
Hants GU11 3HR,
England

and

Gower Publishing Company,
Old Post Road,
Brookfield,
Vermont 05036,
U.S.A.

British Library Cataloguing in Publication Data

Webb, Ian
 Management buy-out : a guide for the prospective
 entrepreneur.
 1. Corporations–Great Britain–Purchasing
 2. Executives–Great Britain
 I. Title
 658.1'6   HD2741

Library of Congress Cataloguing in Publication Data

Webb, Ian
 Management buy-out.
 Bibliography: P. Includes index.
 1. Consolidation and merger of corporation – United States.
 2. Entrepreneur.
 I. Title
 HD2746.5.W43   1985   658.1'6   84-27940

ISBN 0-566-02519-1

Typeset by
Graphic Studios (Southern) Limited, Godalming, Surrey.
Printed in Great Britain by Biddles Ltd, Guildford, Surrey.

Contents

Preface

I started this book early in 1984 as a guide for someone considering whether to assemble a team and mount a management buy-out. Little had been written on the subject at the time; some of the published sources were not widely available and so practical needs were foremost. However, I also hoped to take the book beyond a practical guide and place the subject of management buy-outs in its historical, political and commercial context. Besides, these topics have several practical implications. Another theme which I wanted to develop was entrepreneurship, a fundamental part of management buy-outs, yet also of widespread interest in its own right. Like management buy-outs, some of the published sources on entrepreneurship are difficult to obtain, even in London.

My findings from practical research have been used extensively to build up some of the topics in this book. To this end, I have interviewed a number of people associated with buy-outs and as a result, certain sections are a complete reflection of current opinions.

Various markets soon became apparent for the book. The corporate employee aspiring to a buy-out remains prominent among the intended readership, but he has been joined by others: the company which is the recipient of a buy-out offer, the company planning a divestment, those involved in venture capital, professional firms, students and academics in commercial and industrial economic faculties; all will find something of interest in these pages. The extent of academic interest is particularly surprising. One banker interviewed has even assembled an excellent reading list for many academic callers who lack information on buy-outs and are trying to find it from some unusual sources.

Some of the help I have received with this book is referred to or acknowledged later in the text, but here I should like to thank my wife, Sue, for numerous suggestions and amendments which greatly improve the final work; John W.E. Wilson of the British Institute of Management without whose help and encouragement the book would never have appeared; other staff members of the British Institute of Management; and Mrs Maxine Cullen who coped most admirably with the typing. Finally, I am most grateful to Alastair Morrison of Investors in Industry PLC, and Jon Pither of Amari PLC who read the manuscript. In the light of their detailed comments, numerous additions and improvements have been made.

Ian Webb

1 Introduction

Management Buy-Out: a definition

The term 'management buy-out' has only been in use for five or six years. It arose in committee within the offices of what is now the ICFC Division of Investors in Industry PLC around 1978–79, spread rapidly outside the company, was taken up by the press and is now used widely to the exclusion of other competing terms.*

'Management buy-out' may be abbreviated to 'buy-out' or occasionally to 'MBO', though the latter term has long been reserved for Management by Objectives

---

* The original Industrial and Commercial Finance Corporation has now gone through two changes of name. Currently it is known as ICFC and forms the core business of the Investors in Industry PLC group. Buy-outs are handled by the ICFC division. The group is still widely referred to simply as ICFC.

1

in many circles. It is used in a catholic sense by the press as referring to the purchase of a firm, part of a firm or some of its assets, by an individual or management team which typically work for the firm. Usually the management team secures voting control of the new organisation. Usually too, most of the finance is secured on the assets or on the equity value of the new organisation, but these conditions are not mandatory. Outside teams can operate, the management team may not obtain voting control, financing methods may differ widely and the scheme of the buy-out can take a variety of forms, yet still the transaction is referred to as a management buy-out. About the only certainty in the current usage of the term is that after the buy-out the organisation is run as a going concern, or at least a strong attempt is made to do so.

The leverage buy-out

The broad equivalent to management buy-out in the US is 'leverage buy-out', a term which refers directly to the type of finance; that is the gearing or leverage on the assets. While apparently the more precise term, leverage buy-out can refer to a different style of deal conducted for asset-stripping, as R. Smith (1981) has pointed out. Thus it can exclude qualities such as going concern, the sense of a continuing trading business, which has become an essential feature of buy-outs as they are understood in the UK.

Some alternative terms

It has been suggested that initiation of the deal by the prospective management team should be an essential quality, but often the difficulty here is in knowing who really has initiated a deal. As pointed out in a later chapter, quite often initiation is from another party, but sometimes it is impossible to tell if this is so without inside information. A comparable objection too, can be made against a minimum total consideration for the deal so as to exclude small buy-outs financed informally.

Various other terms have been used for buy-outs. Prior to 1978 they were known as 'Section 54 deals', a name derived from Section 54 of the Companies Act 1948, a former source of complication. 'Incentive financing' has been proposed as a term applying to large deals where the management team has no chance of gaining voting control, but does have a major stake, say up to 15 per cent of the equity. This term appears to have fallen into relative disuse. Another term, 'management buy-in', is sometimes used for deals where an outside team secures control. However, as all other details can be identical to buy-outs, such deals are not dealt with separately in this book.

Divestment

Recognising the problem of terminology, the Business Graduates Association Study (1980) reviewed various terms and adopted the proposals of P. Gorb (1980) on the terms: demerger, hive-off and spin-off. Alas, almost immediately 'demerger' was adopted by the Finance Act 1980 to refer to the provisions of Section 117, while 'hive-off' and 'spin-off' appear to have been little used. This is to be regretted as they had precise definitions. In this book, the term divestment will be adopted for the activity of the vendor, that is, the closure or sale of all or part of an operation so that it is notably smaller after the transaction. Such a definition excludes routine minor sales of assets.

The origins of the modern buy-out

The buy-out as it is known today is generally accepted as originating in the US with minor deals starting in 1959. These were not widely noticed until 1964 when more names entered the field and the trickle of activity built up, becoming a major business by the late 1960s. Immediately, it may be objected that there was nothing new in this development. There may even be those who reflect that they have seen it all before and buy-outs are merely a new name for an old activity. To a large extent this is so, since businesses have been changing hands down the years and it is possible to cite earlier examples with characteristics similar to current buy-outs. Take some of the professional partnerships, which have survived several generations and cycles of death following life following death. It is clear that fresh partners have been introduced, taken stakes in the organisation and gained control before being replaced themselves. Mostly the process has been gradual, without control passing in a single stroke from one group to another. But there have been examples of situations more akin to a palace revolution, with new partners raising finance for their participation by borrowing, amongst other things, against the perceived value of a partnership share, situations indeed, which resembled current practice in all important respects.

So what changes in recent years justify the new terminology and publicity? Writing of conditions in the US before 1965, A.F. Gargiulo and S.J. Levine (1982) note that buyers with cash, credit and credibility had been acquiring businesses for decades, but their activities were localised firstly to unincorporated businesses, notably in the professions and service industries where the asset backing was low; and secondly, to certain businesses where the assets happened to be easy to borrow against. Property and farming have been two examples of the latter. What was exceptional was an acquisition, with control passing to management, of a going concern in manufacturing or trading with significant assets.

While interviewing financiers in the UK* this author has found a similar picture. Yes, there have been many historic deals from past decades which were not then called buy-outs or even Section 54 deals, but if today's criteria were applied they would certainly have been viewed as management buy-outs, present-day practice differing primarily through the financing approach and arrangements. There were other important differences. The volume of activity was lower and there was little or no publicity. Much of this activity too was associated with unincorporated businesses or with private companies which the proprietor had been unable to sell by other methods. Indeed, ICFC, report that a third of the early deals were in this latter category. Therefore, in contrast with recent experience, there was a relative lack of innovative, progressive deals involving a dash of entrepreneurial flair.

The growth of buy-outs in the US

Another break with past experience has come with the scale of growth in buy-outs. Gargiulo and Levine report that divestment rose from 13 per cent total acquisitions in 1969 to a peak of 42 per cent in 1972, falling slightly the following year before reaching another peak of 54 per cent in 1976. A subsequent fall was followed by yet another rise in 1980, so confirming a countercyclical trend against the economic cycle. Of course, these figures give only part of the picture for the US ignoring as they do the value of divestments, some of which may not have been buy-outs as

---

* See Appendix 1

recognised in the UK. Information is incomplete, but it appears that value has risen substantially, with the buy-out market becoming notable since 1979 for the number of deals with a total consideration above $100 million. Such a high level of activity for so long has influenced public awareness of buy-outs to a point where a report in *Business International* (February 1984) credits 'half the executives in the US' with looking carefully for an acquisition.

The growth of buy-outs in the UK

There was a minor burst of activity in 1969 in the UK, coming just after the peak of a boom in mergers. Several acquisitions had led to disastrous results and so created the conditions for buy-outs with a strongly entrepreneurial character which were directly comparable with numerous, more recent situations. Three of the financiers interviewed by the author first handled a buy-out personally in that year. Subsequently the volume of business fell off and the market returned to its former state; a background of partnership and private company succession business with just the occasional exception. The decisive change came late in 1976 when ICFC began to promote the idea of buy-outs actively. From perhaps a score of deals in 1977, the total rose steadily to a peak variously reported as over 200 in 1981. A slight fall from this level in 1982 was followed by a recovery to roughly the 1981 level in 1983 with preliminary indications of another slight fall in the first half of 1984.

Just over half of these deals by number, though slightly less by value, have been handled by the market leader ICFC. Most have been small by US standards, typically having a total consideration of just over £1 million. A handful of exceptions have been of much greater value. These have included the William Timpson buy-out in 1983 for £40.4 million and the largest to date, the National Freight buy-out in 1981 for £53.5 million. Various reports suggest that larger deals will become increasingly common.

The growth of UK buy-outs; some US influence

Although the history of buy-outs in the UK to date has predominantly been associated with ICFC, there have been some parallel developments elsewhere. In this context, the experience of the Electra House Group, an institutional investor, is particularly interesting for its illustrations of the transfusion of ideas and capital across the Atlantic, a process which has operated both ways.

As a result of a mutual association between Electra and Oppenheimer and Co., a New York investment broker which is active in buy-outs, Oppenheimers began to offer Electra a 10 per cent stake in some of their deals from around 1976. Although the business was very small, it was attractive. However, exchange control was operating and structuring the deals to avoid it was a severe limitation on small amounts, so that several had to be turned down. But what there was of this activity emphasised the dearth of investing houses during this period, from perhaps 1979 to 1982, which could provide UK mezzanine finance* and so helped to inspire Electra's subsequent moves: its direct expansion into buy-out financing and its stake in what is perhaps the nearest equivalent in the UK to date of a US buy-out broker, Candover Investments Ltd, which was started in 1980.

Another strand of development may be traced back to 1973 when the New York investment arm of a UK merchant bank, Charterhouse Group International, started in buy-outs. This was very successful and when

---

* See Chapter 5 for mezzanine finance

a deal came up in 1981 which was too large for them, syndication was offered to Electra. Further deals were offered as a result of this initial success and eventually the two houses started a US company specialising in smaller deals, Mezzanine Capital Corporation.

Buy-outs elsewhere in the world

The US, obviously, is by far the largest buy-out market in the world both by number and value. Elsewhere, the second largest market, again by value and number, is reported to be Canada. In Europe, there is much activity in Holland. Indeed, relative to its size it may be larger than the UK, but in absolute terms it is smaller. The ranking of countries in 1984 is thus:

- United States
- Canada
- United Kingdom
- Germany
- Holland
- Italy
- Belgium
- France

There is very little activity in France at all. French management might by now have heard of the concept of a buy-out as there are cases of overseas subsidiaries being bought from French groups, but within France it is believed that market development must await the removal of legal obstacles.

The performance of buy-outs in the UK

The initial results of research on buy-outs are distinctly encouraging. An early study, reported in *Chief Executive* (December 1982) as being the first on buy-out companies' performance, was carried out by Ridmar Marketing Research during the summer of 1982. This found a favourable reaction from employees, suppliers, customers and competitors. The benefits in nearly every case included the survival of the company and the preservation of jobs. In addition, the general elimination of managerial diseconomies had implications for reduced costs, greater managerial flexibility and buy-out team motivation. The sample size in this study was nineteen.

Some preliminary results from another study have also been reported in the *Sunday Times* (9 October 1983). These are from a larger project at the Department of Industrial Economics, Nottingham University, which is believed to be the only publicly funded research into the subject. Using a sample of 103 buy-outs, the researchers, D.M. Wright and J. Coyne, found that employment fell by 17 per cent initially but later recovered to 95 per cent of its original level. This is a remarkable achievement if, as may be inferred, the time span between buy-out and study was around two years. On sales and profits the general picture was of significant progress:

Sales:

Number	Outcome
40	Substantial sales rise
33	Slight sales rise
16	No change
12	Slight sales fall
2	Major sales fall
Total sample 103	

Profits:

Number	Outcome
58	Greater than expected
11	As expected
34	Less than expected
Total sample 103	

Wider conclusions must await the full report from Wright and Coyne, but nevertheless the information they do give is highly favourable. Even the most adverse figure, the thirty-four companies with profits less than expected, are reporting against a target which in most cases will have been an improvement on historic performance.

Assessing buy-out performance

Performance measures for buy-outs are particularly difficult to devise since they are open to various interpretations. Take employment levels for example. There is no guide as to whether these should fall, reflecting good management and cost cutting, or rise as a result of good management leading towards successful growth. The dilemma is compounded by the low state of business fortunes when many buy-outs occur. Recover from near-disaster to a stable, un-exceptional, normal state and the buy-out is con-sidered successful, yet if such a company is analysed, the exercise need not reveal any outstanding features at all, but merely reflect a mundane business in a stable, normal state. Still further complications are introduced by the raised levels of expectations charac-teristic of many buy-outs. The buy-out team puts up a case for financing and issues some optimistic forecasts and intentions which are a break with past perform-ance. Subsequently the team has to perform against those forecasts and if it undershoots it will not necessarily be doing badly.

Despite all these reservations the financiers inter-viewed by the author, with the exception of ICFC, were questioned on buy-out performance. The results from those who responded indicate that as many as 40 per cent of buy-outs could be exceeding their fore-casts, though there was considerable variation in the replies on this point. There is a closer consensus on the proportion which are disappointments, around 15 per cent, but of this only a minority are failures. ICFC reports a failure rate of 10 per cent, a figure expected to rise to perhaps 20 per cent. This much higher incidence of failures can be attributed to ICFC's longer experience of the market. In particular, only one other financing house can really be considered to have assembled a representative portfolio of buy-outs ahead of the 1979–80 recession. Thus for many purposes it may be premature to draw hard conclusions on performance, while recognising that the results, such as they are, are highly encouraging.

Some factors in the late development of UK buy-outs

Buy-outs are successful in the UK yet, despite the example of the US for twelve or more years, it was not until 1977 that the market really accelerated. There may be surprise why the development did not start earlier and why in particular, the experience of 1969 did not lead to a sustained, growing buy-out market. A variety of factors appear to have been operating.

The inhibiting effect of Section 54

Although numerous financiers were successfully circumventing this piece of legislation so that it was having little effect on buy-outs by the time it was replaced in 1981, its earlier influence had been substantial on the development of the market.

M.A. Weinberg, M.V. Blank and A.L. Greystoke (1979) have pointed out that Section 54 of the Companies Act 1948 was originally introduced in the Companies Act 1929 to counter the type of situation which arises when someone arranges a temporary loan, purchases control of a company and then uses the company's funds to repay the loan with which it was purchased. There are numerous possible variations around this situation and Section 54 was drawn very widely to cover them. The purposes of the section were to protect creditors and minority shareholders against the dilution of assets, to protect shareholders generally against directors and to inhibit takeover bids by those of dubious financial standing.

The section was notoriously unsuccessful in achieving its intended objects. As Sir Alexander Johnson (1980) has shown, a combination of other legislation and the adoption of the City Take-over Code in 1969 did much to overcome the problems with minorities, creditors and objectionable take-over practices without any assistance from Section 54. Even after the appearance of the take-over code, there were several instances, over the five years to 1974, of transactions which may or may not have been within the letter of Section 54 but which certainly contravened the original spirit of the Companies Act 1929. After all, in the cycle of raising finance, making a take-over, stripping out the assets and repaying the finance, there need be but few complications to the transactions to obscure the source of the repayment in an accounting sense, let alone in a legal sense. Section 54 was normally only used when fraud was involved and the maximum penalty was a derisory £100. It was no deterrent to a determined market operator.

However, the effects of the section were felt by the banks. As the status of loans could be jeopardised if a borrower became involved in a situation covered by the widely-drawn Section 54, it was perhaps the one section of the Companies Acts which bankers were most anxious to avoid. The consequence was that only exceptional institutions appear to have been able to finance buy-outs and, although their number rose considerably in the late 1970s, the consequent alterations to buy-out schemes to circumvent the legislation made a change desirable. Sections 42-44 of the Companies Act 1981 which replaced Section 54 substantially re-enact the latter's provisions, but with important relaxations for private companies, thus giving significantly more flexibility in the design of buy-out schemes. In the end Section 54 was not actually stopping buy-outs, but earlier it had greatly delayed the development of innovative financing methods.

Some limitations on innovative banking 1970–76

Aside from the special issue of Section 54, the conditions in UK banking in the early 1970s were not conducive to the development of venture capital, of which finance for buy-outs would have been considered a part. Under the newly competitive conditions of the early 1970s, the emphasis of growth was towards markets which could respond rapidly to financing pressures, such as property. Venture capital was not among these markets. There was the memory of losses in the UK through treating venture capital as a straightforward extension of fund management. Few banks had the necessary expertise for financing ventures and it would have taken time to build it up. Between late 1973 and perhaps early 1976, a combination of the secondary banking crisis, rising inflation, the corporate credit squeeze in mid-1974, and the fall in portfolio values towards the end of that year, all helped to create conditions under which innovatory lending was out of the question for nearly all banks.

Venture capital and the purchase by a company of its own shares

Although today it may seem remarkable that expertise in venture capital was so localised only a decade ago, it must be remembered that it was a difficult field in which to make a profit. Finance a company, see it go really well, bring it to the market, then it is easy to realise the capital invested. But with the majority of ventures which are not going to fail, but will never be outstanding either, it is only too easy to get locked into an unmarketable company. With the introduction of Sections 45-62 of the Companies Act 1981, the possibility of a company repurchasing its own shares created a way out for an investor and so greatly raised the attraction of venture capital business, including buy-outs.

Buy-out financing and its rewards

A separate argument for the late development of UK buy-outs is that the rewards are so much greater in the US and that if the position had been similar here the development of buy-outs would have gone ahead irrespective of other factors. Certainly, it is possible to read reports of eight-figure fees for US buy-outs. Even though these are in dollars, the amounts are vastly greater than those currently being received in the UK. For the most part the US fees reflect not only the very much larger buy-outs which are commonplace there, but also it appears that fee proportions are higher in the US as too are fees for all other financial services.

There is room for debate over just how much higher the US fees really are. Typically it is far from clear just what they cover, while estimates of figures in the UK give a total which is lower, but not so much lower, than US levels. A second train of argument maintains that comparison is often virtually impossible. The UK fees may be lower, but the profit is ultimately made in buy-out financing from the equity stakes taken, albeit with a cash flow question for the financier over the years prior to the realisation of the investment. The financiers initial choice of whom to back is made, naturally, with this end in view. In the US, by contrast, much of the business is taken on after an approach by the vendor. Thus at the point of decision for handling the assignment it is often impossible to decide whether the final deal, if any, may be an attractive investment for the buy-out broker. Obviously, there must be a higher front-end fee under such circumstances. Obviously too, this may have to be the pattern in the UK for comparable business, initiated by the vendor, which currently is in its infancy.

Is a comparison with the US valid?

The experience of Electra House already described demonstrates that developments can be influenced from overseas. The early years in the US buy-out market also have a remarkable similarity with the UK; innovative financiers attract others to the business by their example, structural change in the economy leads to much divestment and so buy-outs increase. Could this pattern indicate that subsequent US history will be repeated here?

On the other hand there are some notable differences between conditions in the two countries of which the climate of political and social support for small businesses is possibly the most important. Arguably, there has never been a time since the US Declaration of Independence when the interests of small farmers, small businessmen, and the ideal of the individual operating independently in the economy, have been far from the centre of politics. At times indeed there has been close, direct influence with political mass support for the consequent policies. Reality may have been at variance with the public images of log cabin, haberdashery business and small-time peanut farm associated with Presidents Jackson, Truman and Carter respectively, but no matter. One result has been a lasting legacy of goodwill and social support for entrepreneurship of which buy-outs are a part.

If there was such a background in the UK it might be possible to advocate a rising market for buy-outs in the confidence that if there is a favourable political will, tax and company legislation would eventually be altered in ways which facilitate the buy-out process. In particular there would then be little likelihood of adverse tax and legal measures being inadvertently introduced. As it is, the history of support for small businesses and entrepreneurship by the current Tory administration is only of a few years standing and a simple view of passing fashion would suggest that they are prime candidates for becoming tired political issues, overlooked and neglected. Fortunately perhaps, the issue is more complicated.

In examining the political background policies which affect or are related to management buy-outs, it is difficult not to be impressed by the broad political support recently seen for entrepreneurship. Prior to the mid-1970s, it is difficult to think of any post-war instance of a small business issue securing political mass-support. At that time the Labour administration's formation of the National Enterprise Board and its assistance towards several workers' co-operatives, notably in motorcycles, may be seen as adventures in the nature of entrepreneurship which arguably, for the first time with this issue, did achieve transient mass support. The fact that these experiments were conducted in the name of worker control* should not obscure the concern for the individual identifying with

---

* An interesting comparison may be made here with the measures of the current Tory administration to promote share incentive schemes to enable individuals to participate in the ownership of business. The administration is different, the political personalities involved are very different and the methods are different too, but some of the objectives are remarkably similar.

and owning a part of the organisation which was his livelihood. The subsequent history of these co-operatives emphasises the difficulty of sustaining interest in such an issue without a steady stream of successful, self-supporting, newsworthy results; a lesson which is no less relevant to current management buy-outs.

Buy-outs and central economic planning

It would be sweeping to assume that the experience of co-operatives will now lead a future Labour administration to take an enlightened view of entrepreneurship, but they have provided grounds for optimism. What would affect buy-outs more directly would be renewed interest in bureaucratic control through central economic planning.

Advocated in the 1930s as a means of promoting efficiency and economic growth whose results could then be channelled towards social ends, it was recognised at the time that planning and organisational methods would first have to be improved, but there was confidence that this could be achieved.

The outstanding case against planning, which was made by F.A. von Hayek (1944), has as its major thesis that central planning would lead to a bureacratic, organisational structure and that it would run an economy less efficiently than otherwise. A similar view, but with a UK orientation, was expressed by J. Jewkes (1947). Their case against central planning in the 1940s remained the outstanding opposing argument when it was attempted by the Labour administration in the 1960s.

The National Plan was launched in the autumn of 1965. Arguments in its favour maintained that, whatever the shortcomings of planning in the past, matters had improved and with the help of new agencies, notably the Ministry of Technology, the National

Economic Development Office and the Industrial Reorganisation Corporation, industry would be restructured and co-ordination between sectors improved, so leading to greater efficiency and growth.

Although the National Plan was informally abandoned around the middle of 1966, its legacy for acquisitions, buy-outs and industrial policies has been substantial. In particular, as it was not formally abandoned, it provided the political endorsement for the merger boom of 1967–68 with all its consequences. Surprising at the time, the boom seems all the more remarkable in retrospect for having occurred under a Labour administration. It would have been simple to stop it by, for example, disallowing capital gains tax relief, on some pretext, for share-for-share deals, since little take-over activity at the time was for cash. That this was not done demonstrates the value of political will behind an aspect of industrial policy.

If indicative planning is attempted again, the arguments will be similar to those in 1965: is central planning a method which leads to greater efficiency or not? If not, then the implication is for less bureacracy with more use of competitive markets, however imperfect; and more divestments of all types, among which will be buy-outs.

Buy-outs and industrial concentration

Apart from the special case of central economic planning, arguments for favouring entrepreneurship and buy-outs can be derived from the history of government policy towards mergers and industrial concentration. The subject has been summarised for most of the post-war period by S. Aaronovitch and M.C. Sawyer (1975). They identify measures to meet a popular concern about monopoly power in a vague sense and more specifically, the anti-monopoly sentiments experienced during the merger waves of 1958–

62 and 1967–68 already referred to. Other Government measures were to promote industrial efficiency and to respond to pressure from firms for the removal of restrictions. In addition, there were the direct effects of nationalisation which will be ignored here. Curiously, the results of these measures led to increased competition for small, marginal businesses and so while reducing monopoly power, actually led to a rise in commercial concentration.

Increasing concentration is a trend the UK has experienced since 1919 at least and it appears to be continuing to this day – L. Hannah and J.A. Kay (1977). For most of this time, including the first twenty-five post-war years, it had been widely assumed to be beneficial on the grounds that concentration implies large firms must be more efficient through having expanded faster than small firms. There have also been widely held conceptual arguments that size achieves economies of scale and international competitive strength, particularly at the time of the UK's entry into the EEC in 1973.

Recently various writers have shown that these concepts need not apply and the fact that they were held for so long may be attributed to the difficulties and ambiguity of measuring monopoly power and efficiency. Concentration ratios, for example, emerge as the best measure for concentration, but concentration itself is a poor indicator of monopoly or of market power. Investigations of profits in the UK show little relationship with concentration, but then monopoly profits will be concealed if a firm has chosen a quiet life instead of maximising returns. Thus these studies at a sectoral level failed to give either a clear endorsement for increasing concentration or to provide a case against it, but by implication steadily helped to raise the question of whether there should be a government policy at all on the matter.

Buy-outs and the future

Against the background of this parlous record of the effects of mergers and acquisitions and related government policy, it is appropriate to question whether there is a realistic prospect of at least ten years of market development for divestments and buy-outs. Without being over-optimistic, this appears to be the prospect. There are grounds from the initial results of buy-outs for believing that they raise economic efficiency and there is broad political consensus and support for the concept.

'Buy-outs are an intellectual revolution. People who were in comfortable jobs can now see themselves owning and running their own business on a significant scale and with the opportunity to accumulate substantial capital'.

L.R. Blackstone
(Blackstone, Franks, Smith & Co.)

2 Entrepreneurship and the buy-out

The conversion of a corporate mentality to the entrepreneurial mentality is a major source of difficulty and the biggest trauma the buy-out team will face. It can take a couple of years before the whole team has adjusted to owning and running a business.

N. Falkner
(Development Capital Group Ltd)

Why study entrepreneurship?

The vast majority of buy-out team members will have been employees of organisations all of their working lives and now will be considering independence for the first time. Most will have some misgivings at the prospect of becoming an entrepreneur. The change in functions, duties, and reporting relationships; the alterations to the perception of their posts and the ways they are perceived by others, all contribute to uncertainty, to anxiety. Central to these doubts may be a sense of ignorance over what an entrepreneur is. What after all are the key features of the entrepreneurial role and what, if anything, can be done in advance to adjust to them?

Outside the buy-out team, there will be numerous parties interested in entrepreneurship and the nature of the entrepreneurial psychology. Financiers, accountants, lawyers, even academics and politicians, all can justify more than a passing interest in the subject. Their outstanding purpose will be to assess the organisation as a whole, of which the entrepreneurial functions are just a part. As will be covered in Chapter 4, in most cases financiers screening a proposition judge the buy-out team first and the business second. The emphasis is very much on isolating competent management capable of working independently. Naturally, this process focuses attention on entrepreneurship, a quality which must be seen in at least one team member.

Further reasons for studying entrepreneurship are provided by the importance of this leading personality. Through decisions on strategy, capital investment and choice of key personnel, it is possible for one individual to set a style whose effects last for years; frequently indeed, for long after the decision-taker has departed. This influence can be readily observed in large, newsworthy, public corporations, and on occasions matters such as a major take-over battle place the issue in sharp relief. Life is less dramatic in smaller, private companies and it is notably more difficult to assess and analyse, but there are grounds for believing that here the relative influence of the proprietor is even greater; that in many ways his business becomes a reflection of his personality.

Entrepreneurship is recognised as a critical factor in

assembling information for a buy-out yet comparatively little has been published on the subject relative
to other aspects of commerce. Questions on matters
such as why and how people innovate, take risks, start
businesses or new activities and then build up a
substantial organisation may seem central to the
national economy, yet they have received limited
attention. Where these and related topics are covered,
entrepreneurship often emerges as an elusive
phenomenon. At fault here are some seemingly
pedantic points of definition over entrepreneurial
qualities and types. Often the entrepreneurial function
is imprecise and portrayed as including activities which
those from corporations will recognise as purely
managerial. Alternatively, a definition may be taken
which concentrates on just one entrepreneurial
quality, such as risk-taking, to the exclusion of other
possible qualities. From such limited standpoints it is
possible to handle the subject of entrepreneurship
within a corporate framework and so overlook entirely
the problems introduced by an entrepreneur operating independently of a corporation. Define entrepreneurs more carefully to include independent businesses as well as some corporate roles and still the
buy-out team is open to confusion, for the over-
whelming majority of the sample will consist of firms
employing only a few employees; businesses which
will always stay small and so have little or nothing in
common with the style of organisation involved in
nearly all buy-outs.

To attempt to resolve some of the difficulties, and
place the subject of entrepreneurship in its appropriate perspective, a review of some of the literature
on the place of the entrepreneur in economics and in
entrepreneurial psychology appears in Appendix 3.
Much of the theory and research on entrepreneurship
is complicated and will go beyond the immediate
purposes of the prospective buy-out team member.

Therefore for the reader whose aims are essentially practical, there is a case for concentrating on a summary of some of the more important points which appear in the remainder of this chapter.

The implications from the theory and research on entrepreneurship may be divided broadly between who the entrepreneurs are and what they are, in the sense of what are their abilities, motivations and characteristics. Naturally the two are interdependent in large measure, origins and past career having at least some influence on the current profile. Three factors emerge as influencing the creation of entrepreneurs.

Educational, social and occupational backgrounds

Although the higher ranks of corporations tend to be staffed by persons from certain social and higher educational backgrounds with a corporate career pattern, the picture among entrepreneurs is notably more diverse. A disadvantaged social or educational background need be no barrier to entrepreneurship.

Previous association with small businesses and other entrepreneurs

New entrepreneurs are frequently generated from among those who associate with entrepreneurial activity. Various contacts can be relevant. A parent who is self-employed, other members of the family or friends working in small businesses, being employed by a small business oneself; all have been shown to raise substantially the chance of becoming an entrepreneur.

Minority groups membership

It is not necessary to be a member of a disadvantaged minority group to become an entrepreneur, but it

does increase, the probability of becoming an entrepreneur.

Some comments are needed on these points.
Although higher educational and social backgrounds
have been shown to be an advantage for those
climbing a corporate ladder, but less so for successful
entrepreneurship, more research is needed on the
particular needs of a buy-out team where background
and ability may have been crucial in team selection.

The statistical correlation between the generation of
entrepreneurs and some previous association with
entrepreneurial activity is sufficiently marked as to be
virtually beyond question. However, it leaves un-
answered the probability that many will never become
entrepreneurs, no matter how much exposure they
have to small businesses and other entrepreneurs.
Also relevant to buy-outs, but not yet researched, is
whether a promising entrepreneurial personality who
joins a corporation can become so conditioned by the
innumerable, specific features of corporate life as to
be incapable of subsequent entrepreneurial activity.
Such a negative factor might be helping to contribute
towards what appears, at first sight, to be a clear
relationship between new entrepreneurs and their
historic association with entrepreneurship.

Though minority groups may play only a small part in
buy-outs, their importance to entrepreneurship in a
wider sense may indicate that there is something of
value to be learned from them.

Some of the characteristics and motivations of entrepreneurs

Independence

Many of those who are attracted by entrepreneurship
are personalities who thrive on independence.

Management succession

Experience proves that some of those who wish to avoid the control of others, tend to dominate the organisations they create. Immediately this introduces the danger of poor organisational development and an incipient succession problem.

Achievement motivation

Nearly everyone who breaks away from a large organisation ends up running a very small business; small garages, workshops, retail outlets; businesses which have always seemed small and always will. A few distinguish themselves from this majority by forming major businesses, and the buy-out team leaders must be among this group. The outstanding motivation has been variously described, but will be termed here as 'achievement'. Researchers have associated other personal characteristics with this type of motivation, among them:

- Activity in community affairs.
- Dislike of repetitive, routine work.
- Resistance to social pressures.
- Choice of experts as working partners in preference to friends.

Behaviour towards risk-taking by those with high achievement motivation is particularly interesting. Typically a moderate risk is chosen, which can be reduced through work, in preference to either a high risk with an outside chance of high return, or a low risk with little challenge. Gambling, in the sense of operating a risk situation at which eventual loss is inevitable, tends to be avoided, being a characteristic activity of those with low achievement motivation.

Personal backgrounds

In contrast to the ordered lives of most corporate

career employees, many entrepreneurs have experienced fluctuating fortunes and in consequence have had to adjust their aims, aspirations and social contacts to meet the changed situation. This point alone should cause managers in a corporate environment to reconsider carefully their suitability for participation in a buy-out team.

Job creation as a motive

Issues of social welfare often lie behind government industrial policies. The type of personality which survives the trauma of independence and runs a business successfully, has little or no regard for such matters.

The money motive

Though dominant for most employees, the money motive has been found to play only a minor role in entrepreneurial motivation.

Perhaps the outstanding observation to be made from this brief summary is of the several departures from a common-sense view. True, it can be reasoned that entrepreneurs may thrive on independence and may wish to do little or nothing to promote job creation as a prime aspect of policy, but elsewhere the literature on the subject has some radical implications. Management succession problems sound obvious in theory, but in practice their symptoms may be difficult to recognise. The diffuse inefficiency; the demoralised personnel gossiping among themselves and being gossiped about in a derogatory manner by an entrepreneur for whom control is crucial, so preventing the emergence of suitable support and a more open style of direction; these consequences and more may be related to personality characteristics, widespread among some entrepreneurs, acquired long before the present phase of their business careers.

It is on motivational issues however that the entrepreneur diverges most markedly from mundane practice. It a straw poll is taken of employees on motivation, the great majority see themselves at work for money and nothing else. An academic viewpoint would soften this conclusion by questioning the extent to which money matters and then might offer any or all of the several theories of motivation based on a corporate framework. While recognising that these theories offer a state in which coercion, physical needs and money certainly operate, another state can be reached in which motivation by means of higher management qualities becomes paramount. That the former is the more common situation in practice may be inferred from the relative proliferation of case studies involving its features. In displaying low money motivation and having additional characteristics such as achievement, the entrepreneur who succeeds in running a substantial business may be isolated as an exceptional person.

3 Buyouts and the divesting company

Recent history in the UK has perhaps shown the divesting organisation in an unfavourable light. The economic downturn of 1979–80 followed by substantial recovery, but with very low growth, exacerbated many of the factors which eventually led to buy-outs and so placed exposure on corporate efficiency. But irrespective of the economic conditions, there does seem to have been an air of desperation about rather too many UK buy-outs – sales completed at prices well below notional market values of not so long before, often for hasty reasons, reflecting poor management or the next best alternative to liquidation. How much more preferable it might have been for the divesting organisation if a measure of forward planning had led to a more ordered pace of events and an attempt to choose the opportune time for a sale.

Hitherto there appear to be few examples of buy-outs in the UK in which the divesting company has taken any initiative except against a background of distress. Not all buy-outs result from a distressed situation, but nearly all exceptions involve subsidiaries which have become foot-loose for reasons which, on closer appraisal, tend to reflect unfavourably on the parent company. Many corporations may wish to avoid this unsatisfactory state of affairs.

In the US the position is often more formal. A corporation adopts thoroughgoing planning methods and develops them over time. As a direct result, proposals for acquisitions and divestments are produced in committee and a professional firm of buy-out brokers is engaged to assess the suitability of the divestment for a buy-out, or for an alternative method of disposal. Many ideas may never get beyond this stage; the divestment may prove to be inadvisable on grounds of broad strategy; it may not form a viable, independent unit; the corporation's views on its value may be irreconcilable with reality; or there may be no one around whom an effective team can be built. For these and many other reasons the divestment option may be deferred for the current year. The buy-out broker charges a fee and the corporation benefits from an external criticism of its planning and strategy, so creating a stronger base from which to conduct the exercise in future years.

On the other hand, some divestment proposals will be suited to a buy-out. When this happens the broker isolates a group of employees, relays the proposition, encourages them to form a team and helps them to mount a buy-out. From there the procedure is similar to UK buy-out practice, except that the negotiations are with a benign vendor who typically has a direct interest and a financial stake in the new venture.

An important condition for this active divestment process in the US is the general encouragement for ventures already noted in Chapter 1. It is well known that only about one in four or five new start-ups will even survive to ten years, and the proportion meeting most peoples' ideas of success is much smaller still. Necessarily, allowance must be made for disappoint- ments if the process as a whole is to be promoted. This attitude is carried over to some of the riskier aspects of corporate life; so long as there is an acquisition policy and a strategy review there are bound to be misfits, disappointments, or merely ideas which do not work out as originally intended. Divestments are just one part of commercial life which present their own set of opportunities. By contrast, a corporation's attitude towards divestments in the UK is often one of a possible failure which the corporation would prefer to avoid by not divesting.

Notwithstanding this difficulty, US-style divestment activity has taken root in the UK and examples are reported, at least at the enquiry stage. Promotion of the approach is already under way and significant developments may be expected. As a result, there is much value in examining the characteristics of the divestment decision and the planning process of which it is a part.

Planning and divestment

There are many UK organisations which have used planning for years. Indeed, it was among subsidiaries of overseas companies, multinationals and the larger UK corporations that the Business Graduates Associa- tion's Survey of divestment (1980) found the most progressive attitudes. Multinationals, for example, are often liberal and recognise the value of divestment in tidying up a company. Other large commercial and trading companies also have a favourable attitude and tradition towards buying and selling companies, recognising employees as another potential customer. But in production companies, which are judged by the study as having the most to gain from active divestment, there was far less enthusiasm for an idea which was frequently viewed as an admission of failure. Significantly, these are organisations where progressive management techniques may have been attempted, but inadequately developed.

In considering what planning might achieve for an organisation it may be valuable, firstly, to distinguish those factors which can lead to divestment. A survey in the US and Europe by J.J. Boddewyn (1976) identified the following:

- Specialised management needs
- Remote geographical location
- Lack of strategic fit
- Problems elsewhere in the company
- Bad management
- Bad acquisitions
- Low growth and poor prospects

Any or all of these factors may apply and several can be expected to be inter-dependent, so complicating any analysis or attempt to disentangle cause and effect. In such a situation, the planning approach must be comprehensive if such broad factors are to be covered. The approach must also have been established for some time to be fully effective. Several of these factors will typically be expressed by a cash flow crisis for which, in the final instance, planning can do little. Rather, its causes had to be anticipated well in advance for the crisis to be avoided.

Planning in the small business

In many businesses it may be totally misleading to consider planning for divestment when planning has never been part of that company's policy. This situation is most frequently encountered in small organisations and in those which, though larger, are essentially run as a small business with simple lines of authority and control centred on the proprietor. Here formal planning methods have little chance of being adopted, since it is rare that they can be justified on their current return, or even on a two year view. If the proprietor could anticipate activity any further ahead, he would probably be planning already. As it is, the considerable time and trouble needed for the initial introduction of formal planning methods is never made.

For organisations of this nature, there are no ready answers. Much of the confusion arises because planning within organisations is not itself a solution to problems but merely a way towards solutions. It involves assembling historic information, current aims and forecasts, and structuring them so that they are co-ordinated and consistent. This process can reveal shortcomings and improve the basis from which discretionary choices are made. Typically it does so.

The time horizon

The style of planning adopted may differ markedly between organisations, because the factors for which viable forecasts can be made will vary, as too will the businessmen actually making the forecasts.

The procedure, however, may be similar, if only to minimise the substantial re-working of the plan as its implications start to emerge. Initially it is necessary to assess which relevant factors can be forecast and for how far ahead. At this stage the assessment should only be made in general terms. The detail will be needed later, but it is consequent upon the actual budgets which are drawn up and these go beyond the needs of planning for divestment. Nonetheless, it is possible from a general appraisal to isolate the time span over which the forecasts and plan will operate. Great variety must be expected; certain pieces of financial information have a time horizon of less than a day, while issues concerning operations, personnel and marketing, involve forecasts which can extend to a matter of years. In most corporations, a three to four year time span is a working reality for new products, new markets, premises and matters concerning the workforce.

The mission and objectives

Having isolated a time horizon from the provisional forecasts, it is desirable to establish objectives and a mission for the company. These comprise a set of hopes, aims and intentions which are feasible, yet challenging, towards which the company will move. They should range beyond the time horizon of the forecasts as they will later help to structure them. The mission and objectives should refer to all major aspects of the business and may be detailed on matters such as market share, product range, premises, production facilities, and size of workforce. Concepts may be introduced with only a general implication. For example, an objective could be to match the costs of the most efficient major competitor. What matters is that all necessary policies are implied as consequences of the mission and objectives. Certain major divestments could be targeted as objectives, but this would be exceptional.

The strategy and policies

Though simple in outline, the strategy and policies by which the mission and objectives will be attained can lead to much elaborate work. They introduce the need for a position audit of the current organisation, with much detail on subsidiaries, and can even involve a performance review of major assets. It is at this stage that the question of divestment is most likely to arise, either on the grounds of relative performance or

through some obvious mismatch between facilities
and objectives. However, there are dangers in drawing
conclusions too soon. As measures and policies are
designed to meet objectives some of the latter are
virtually certain to be revealed as unattainable, so
leading to a lengthy process of revision and reformula-
tion of the earlier planning stage.

Expanding the planning process

The assembly of information and opinion will have
drawn many people into the discussion and in most
companies this is an essential feature of the planning
process. The survey of divestment by J.J. Boddewyn
(1976) found that the initial decision to divest usually
originated in a middle-level operating unit, thereby
emphasising the importance of opening up the planning debate. However, just who and what is to be
included may be a delicate matter. The danger with an
issue such as divestment, is of creating a group with a
personal interest very early on, at a time when
precedence is needed for the interests of shareholders, directors, other personnel and the continuing
operation of the business. In addition, it may not be in
anyone's interest to anticipate a conclusion too early.
The various ideas generated during the planning
process may later be rejected as budgets are
developed from the policies and the full implications
become readily apparent. Besides, the actual decision
to divest may only be taken at a periodic review of the
corporate plan by an appropriate level of authority.

The emergence of a buy-out

Perhaps the first question in connection with a probable divestment is whether it appears to form a viable,
self-supporting unit. If it does, the choice of divestment methods is wider and should include a buy-out.

Once a decision is taken, the divestment process will speed up. The survey by J.J. Boddewyn (1976), found that the average time between the decision to divest and completion was eleven months, within a range of three months to two years. During the period devoted to negotiation, there may be implications for the competitive position of the rest of the organisation, for customer goodwill and for various practical matters such as internal overhead allocation.

In many situations, a buy-out will not only be feasible, it will also be the preferable course of action for the divesting organisation. The lack of an external buyer, difficulties over price and valuation, the need for significant management expertise essential for the business and hard to replace at short notice, strong local affiliations and a potential redundancy liability are all reasons why a buy-out may be the favoured divestment method. Much however will depend on whether a suitable prospective buy-out team is available. Engineering a buy-out may simply involve dropping a hint to the potential team, but if such a team is not ready to emerge, there is little more which can be done at short notice. In most cases it is doubtful whether much more can be done even with the advantage of time. It is theoretically possible to appoint appropriate staff and delegate the buy-out to them, but often a decision of this nature is at the heart of managerial shortcomings. If the organisation had been progressive and efficient, the issue of divestment would probably never have arisen.

Share options and incentives

One measure which might be worth considering to help build up future buy-out teams is a share-incentive or save-as-you-earn share option scheme. It is often uncertain exactly what function these schemes are intended to perform. As noted in Chapter 6, they are unlikely to be used to gain control of a company and most employees would probably prefer a salary rise as motivation. In addition, with the individual already relying on one source for an income and a pension, there is a major risk in investing in the same organisation. No professional fund manager could survive with such poor portfolio diversification. However, by introducing many people to the ownership of equities, they might help to prepare a team for a buy-out. There is widespread prejudice bordering on hostility towards risk-taking, towards the Stock market and the City in general which must be overcome by the buy-out team, yet which often can only be dispelled carefully over time. A share incentive scheme could help in this process and so play a part in adjusting corporate employees to the idea of owning and running a business. Further information is given in Chapter 6.

The initial offer arrives

Although this chapter has been concerned mainly with advance planning for divestment, there will be many organisations which will never have considered the possibility prior to the arrival of the initial offer. In other cases there will be surprise over the exact timing of the offer. Initially it is necessary to decide who is to know about it, to see that they are informed and to decide whether there is a conflict of interest in the buy-out team continuing to perform their salaried jobs. Once these matters are in hand an assessment of the offer may be made. This assessment is likely to be affected by several general conditions:

- Is the current offer a competent offer?
- What are the alternatives?
- Is the price within a range at which negotiation could start?
- Will a competitive bid be needed?
- Whose agreement will be needed for a sale?

The competence of the offer will reflect the standing of the buy-out team and whether they appear to be able to finance it. If the terms of the offer are likely to be changed radically once negotiations have started it is advisable to consider whether finance would still be forthcoming. It may be in everyone's interest to expose a lack of credibility as soon as possible.

Some issues in taking a buy-out offer to completion

The possibility of an alternative to the current offer hinges partly on the difference between the offered price and the market value of the subsidiary or assets in question. These will be the subject of a detailed investigation, so the issue of a competitive bid essentially remains open until completion, but initially a provisional estimate must at least hold the prospect of ultimate satisfaction to all parties, otherwise an alternative must be sought. In this event, there must be the probability that if an attractive offer is received from another party it will both be accepted and taken to completion.

Various personal issues can affect the outcome either way and are highly important. The organisation may wish to see an established workforce continue in employment under a known leadership rather than risk uncertain direction. Yet, on the other hand, individuals within the organisation may be reluctant to lose control of the buy-out team and see them gain power, autonomy and the prospect of wealth. Intense jealousies can arise with the result that some corporate officers would rather sell to an outsider bidder at virtually any price than to the buy-out team. Many complications of this kind are possible and tend to involve irrational motives, when the best interests of the divesting organisation are usually best served by rational decisions based on figures and facts.

The decision-taking capability of the divesting

organisation can be a further source of inefficiency and obstruction. Rapid decisions are needed on the many terms and price changes which often occur before an agreement in principle is reached with the bidder. To this end it is important to decide early on who will actually be taking the final decision on whether to sell, and on what price and terms. This decision is perhaps more valuable to the bidders, who have more commitment than the vendor to the outcome, but it is not as though there is no commitment at all on the part of the vendor and it increases steadily the longer negotiations are in progress. The vendor's time and trouble will arise principally from a detailed appraisal of the divestment. Here someone will be working over much the same ground as the buy-out team and it may be inadvisable to rely solely on information which has come from or been influenced by team members. The alternative is to use external advice.

4 Achieving a buy-out

The outline of the proceedings

In outline, the steps to be taken towards achieving a buy-out are simple. The idea for the possibility of a buy-out emerges; a provisional team comes together and decides with the aid of a brief, often informal, business plan that the venture is viable, and that the team can manage it. They then judge whether the present owner will sell if presented with a realistic offer and approach financiers to get an indication of whether finance is likely to be feasible. Following favourable responses, professional advisers are engaged, a complete business plan is produced and an initial offer made to the vendor. Having secured a provisional agreement with the vendor, the finance can be arranged in detail. This then allows final agreement to be reached with the vendor, financial arrangements are completed, the vendor is paid and at last the deal is completed.

Any or all of these stages can be vastly more complicated, while confusion can be introduced by elaboration of the negotiations, often as a result of disagreement. In addition the order of the various steps is only an outline; professional advice can be taken at the outset, team formation can be delayed as too can the construction of the main business plan. However, it is precisely because of the variation, complexity, uncertainty and time over which the proceedings are structured that the relatively simple objectives of the exercise should not be overlooked.

The idea for the buy-out

Buy-outs may be considered as starting when someone has the idea that the possibility of a buy-out is worth considering. Most ideas fade before leading to any significant practical steps, either through a lack of application or because the project clearly fails to cohere as a promising enterprise. But of those which survive, many have evidently remained as ideas for a long time and many too have not actually come from the buy-out team, points which suggest a prospective entrepreneur should be patient while seeking his opportunity. It is impossible to estimate how many buy-outs actually originate outside the final buy-out team. Sales from receivers and some conscious divestments can be identified, such as those from the public sector, and in nearly all these cases a team member has been approached with a broad propostion. Less easy to isolate, though, are the informal approaches within corporations, often no more than a discreet hint over a drink that the parent organisation might consider a sale. The signs can be quite insignificant but they are frequently there to be exploited.

The question of who produced the idea, and how

and when it was produced, can have considerable bearing on the next step which is to decide whether the team is likely to have the makings of a deal. In a sense this decision continues right through to completion, as commitments of enthusiasm, time and trouble from everyone concerned increase steadily. At the start, however, the decision is of a different nature, being taken on incomplete information in a situation where the chances of an unfavourable outcome are high. Some recipients of ideas, particularly where there has been an approach from a receiver, will find it desirable to take professional advice very early on from someone experienced in buy-outs. From the vantage of a detached, unemotional viewpoint the adviser can broadly assess the vendor, the business, the prospective buy-out team and financial possibilities. Others, especially those with much time available, may prefer to investigate these matters themselves.

The vendor's attitude

The idea has arisen, the buy-out team is right, the business is promising, and there is every indication of finance. Is this the outstanding opportunity of your business career? Probably not, unless you have a willing vendor. There is room for subjective judgement over reasons for failing; a selling price pitched too high can express a variety of motives as well as a genuine, well-rooted conviction over the value of a business. Nevertheless, in discussion with financiers who expressed a view on the subject, it appears that of those buy-outs considered in some depth at the financing stage, roughly half are abandoned, or otherwise fail, because the vendor is unwilling to sell. It is therefore likely that an even higher proportion are eliminated for this reason earlier on.

There are many reasons for unwilling vendors and

there will be scope in some cases for buy-out teams to anticipate the problem and work around it. Price and valuation are obvious causes but at least they lead to clear-cut financial calculations and a financing issue. More difficult to handle are companies to which a buy-out is a novelty and the decision-taking function is obscure; or where a minority of executives are enthusiastic, promote the idea to a team but are then outvoted by other executives who may have little or no direct interest in the subsidiary concerned. Some real problems can also arise over taxation issues and to a great extent it is up to the buy-out team to anticipate such matters. Many prospective teams spend several months carefully assessing the obstacles and attempting to influence attitudes favourably towards a possible buy-out ahead of giving any indication of their actual motives. In many companies, careers can be jeopardised if employees are found to be planning a buy-out.

Another source of difficulty with vendors concerns the personality problems which can emerge over the issue of divestment. These can accelerate once negotiations are under way. Jealousy of prospective independence, envy of the capital others have raised and may shortly make, loss of power and authority; all these and more can come into play and it is essential they be anticipated and forestalled. The process can start early on by identifying friends at court, such as board members who can be counted upon for support against a personal difficulty, and also by isolating sources of hostility. D.S. Haggett (1981) has termed an objector about to lose power as 'the man in the yellow trousers' and he may be expected in most buy-outs. Typically, though not always, he is the man to whom the buy-out team report and his early identification is essential.

One advantage of buying from a receiver is that you have at least a willing vendor. Regrettably, that is about the only advantage since receivers tend to encourage counter-bids to which they are nearly always open. All too often a contested situation develops under pressure of time with a vendor who lacks those historic ties with the business and workforce which can influence some of the final terms. Similarly, deals promoted by the vendor can have their disadvantages. There is a seller, but why? Everyone has heard of successful buy-outs in which the team makes money. Much less is heard of the unsuccessful minority of buy-outs where the vendor, in retrospect, is very pleased with the price obtained or where subsidiaries were promoted to buy-out teams whose capabilities were inadequate. They are not totally unknown. This is not to advise undue caution but merely appropriate diligence on a delicate subject.

Relations between the vendor and the buy-out team are likely always to remain an anomalous situation. The allegiance of the team members has been towards a corporation which has advanced their careers, but now they are starting to work in a contrary manner. At some point in the proceedings, the balance of the team's activities will be towards their self-interest and away from the vendor, who nonetheless faces the prospect of paying their salaries for an indeterminate number of months and may meanwhile be unable to work towards their replacement. Naturally, a hostile development of this nature can have unpredictable results. To this end, it is advisable to assess when the team may be considered to be working against the corporation and when it will be seen to be hostile.

The viability of the business

Initially, this question will need little attention. The buy-out team are likely to be quite the most knowledgeable group on the subject and this will be demonstrated later when a full business plan is constructed. However, there can be pitfalls in long-standing acquaintance with an activity. Technology which has been irredeemably superseded is the type of issue an outsider might see more clearly and question accordingly. There are also conditions, such as drastic rationalisation, which someone with no pre-conceived ideas about the business can handle more effectively. The need is to question what the team will do with the business which has not been done already and then assess rapidly whether the venture is sound and viable.

The formation of the buy-out team

Nearly all buy-out teams start with just one person and some remain so right through to completion. These, however, form rather less than 10 per cent of all buy-outs; a figure which includes those persons who say they have a team, but which on investigation is found to have no equity. Many teams are dominated by one personality, but these must be distinguished from one-person teams because they have accepted co-directors with important equity stakes. Teams are mostly formed prior to the initial offer to the vendor though membership can change during negotiations. Yet even in this case the association of the members is made while the objective is to achieve a buy-out, an objective whose motivation and pressures may differ from the team's traditional experience and from their experience after the buy-out.

Pressure to form a team, if there is not one already, will almost invariably come from the financiers. The reason for this, as A. Mills and P. Miles (1984) have indicated, is that the fundamental reason for a buy-out failing lies with management whose narrow expertise and career within a large group is suddenly inadequate to the wider demands of a smaller but autonomous business. Increase the numbers in the team and much of the problem will be solved. A certain minimum size of business is thus required to support a team large enough to include a full complement of commercial skills. Those with the information and acumen to survive alone are few, and the high casualty rate among new start-ups which cannot support a team may be related to this point.

Financiers have emphasised the over-riding importance of a team's calibre many times; an excellent team can run any business. At times it even seems the business itself can be neglected, so long as the people are right. Underlying the financier's concern is the knowledge that while most things can be put right with a business relatively quickly, team changes are difficult, slow and liable to jeopardise the whole enterprise. Although the members will have worked together, often for many years, a buy-out subjects them to a new experience and mistakes can usually be traced back to the early days of team formation.

Weaknesses in the buy-out team tend to surface in two ways. Firstly, there are those who fail during the negotiation and thereby endanger the outcome for everyone else. Because there is great uncertainty, an indeterminate timescale, personal financial commitments and several adversaries, it is hardly surprising that numerous financiers have referred to the attrition and toll experienced by team members. But stress is not the only factor. Team members often take their hierarchy from their current organisational positions with the result that latent qualities of leadership emerging from a junior member can destabilise the group. Other symptoms of inappropriate leadership can arise once completion is in sight and attention turns away from the job in hand towards equity shares. D. Michaels (1983) has referred to this as the 'greed-ometer factor'; a most destructive influence which can reduce a team to a group of squabbling individuals.

The second category of team member failures occurs after the buy-out. There are new functions, responsibilities and pressures to which it is necessary to adjust at a time of heavy work-load. Above all there is the lack of an established organisation and the general trauma of independence to which full adjustment can take up to two years. Opinions and experiences vary considerably on the incidence of team member replacement after buy-outs, but there seems to be little doubt over the difficulty which can arise in removing an equity holder from office unless he has chosen to go, or over the debilitating effects on the company which occur after any event of this nature.

So the prudent team leader looks ahead and selects the members accordingly. Unfortunately the task is complicated by the limited choice of team members which is typically available. Usually, a team size of two to five members is desirable, containing a balance of skills. The leader should have entrepreneurial characteristics and, if the other members have too, then so much the better. Of the actual disciplines to be included, there are compelling arguments for including the finance director. Normally he is the easiest man to replace after a buy-out since accounts functions differ far less widely between companies than other departmental functions. Besides, the professional firms can cover for in-house services at short notice should this be really necessary. Conditions before a buy-out, however, can be expected to be totally different to normal. Information on tax, accounts, corporate legal and company secretarial matters are the very currency of buy-outs and most of these topics are the preserve of the finance director. The pressure on the accounts department for innumerable statements and schedules is such that additional staff are advisable, and the problems which can arise if the department is unfriendly should not be forgotten. It frequently happens that the holder of some important office is personally unsuitable for the buy-out team and under such circumstances it is preferable to postpone a plan rather than incur a mistake. Even in the early stages, team members can be very difficult to drop.

While under pressure from the financiers to form a team it is important to remember that an essential part of their screening of the financing application will consist simply of judging that team. Traditional methods are used almost universally for this purpose with the team judged for its competence, motivation, cohesion and general ability to run the venture they are proposing. Past backgrounds and the contents of the business plan are both very important sources of information on the team. Between fifteen to twenty personal reference checks on the team members as a whole will be made by the lead financier.

The initial financing outline

Much information will be needed for a full financing proposal, and few teams will want to make such a heavy, speculative commitment to an idea which at this stage is more than likely to come to nothing. The solution is to obtain an indication of the likelihood of financing which provides justification for the necessary measures to support a first offer to the vendor. Contrary to the traditional view of the mystique of banking, some financiers have stressed how very easy it is to obtain this initial indication on financing possibilities. All you need to do is to contact them by telephone giving the facts of the situation and the approximate price. It is then possible to say whether a meeting is justified.

Of course, this is a view from the banker's side of the desk. It presupposes that the applicant can identify the salient facts of the situation, knows whom to telephone in which bank and then just happens to catch the banker at the right time of the day. In practice while some bankers are approachable, others are less so. Some major banks have little or nothing to do with buy-outs; others go through phases when they are investing little in buy-outs and it is difficult for an outsider to get up-to-date information on these points. Applications to unsuitable quarters can lead to replies which are interpreted as indicating fault with the project, when the real reason for refusal is something totally different. Accordingly, it is recommended that the names of two banks are found which are known to be highly active in buy-outs and initial applications be made to just those two and one other name. If all three are negative, take some professional advice if you have not done so already, and re-examine the project before applying to more.

The development of divestments in the UK is inhibited by the current state of the law of enticement. If the financier offers finance freely and with initiative he can be open to an action for enticement from the parent company. This can apply in particular where part of the business is lost before the buy-out and where employees other than the buy-out team move away. The law can be circumvented, but until there is a clear indication of a willing vendor, it is a caveat and this is within a banking sector which, with very few exceptions, lacks a tradition of imaginative marketing. The emphasis on verbal assurances, with little or no documentation, in the early stages might be attributed to this cause. But such matters recede once there is a willing vendor.

Using professional advisers

With preliminary and encouraging indications on the vendor, business, team and financing, the way will be clear to pursue the commitment and, almost inevitably, this will include engaging professional advisers.

Some teams will have found advisers early on, but most tend to delay such a move until the views and attitudes of financiers on the team and the venture have started to become conditioned. Such a pattern is regrettable when it is remembered that ultimate success will depend to a great extent on employing and using good professional advice.

An initial handicap for many in commerce may be the dowdy image professional people all too often have in smaller low-growth organisations and in branches of corporations. Frequently they are only employed on matters such as debt-collection, audits and routine tax, and the mundane impression is rarely dispelled by the occasional larger report on something such as organisational issues or management accounts. Much of the relevance of what they are doing can be disputed; much of the detail seems superfluous. In the end, for some unaccountable reason, no one from the organisation quite manages the inspiration to ask the questions which really would use outside help for progressive purposes. Instead, reports are shelved, fees are paid, and life goes on. When a buy-out is in prospect, the past must be forgotten and a very different style of professional adviser should be engaged and used imaginatively. Understandably, there may be some initial reluctance over the move.

Another inhibition over approaching professionals for help wiill be uncertainty over the expense and the possibly high proportion which may fall on the buy-out team personally. Part of the difficulty lies in not knowing exactly how much help will be needed and for what purposes; but even if this is known precisely there may be obscurity at the outset over the fee structures. Virtually all buy-outs will need assistance with legal and company secretarial matters, and with tax too. Even if the team has outstanding expertise in some of these areas, it will be necessary to reassure the financiers with an external opinion. Most teams may be expected to need additional help with the accountancy aspects of the business plan and most, too, can benefit from the advice of someone who has been previously involved in buy-outs and can co-ordinate some of the activities, advise on negotiating strategy and so on. Most professionals working on buy-outs can combine several of these functions.

It is essential when choosing professional advisers to engage those who have worked on buy-outs before. Advice on whom to approach is available from several quarters, including the financiers, and teams should not be afraid to approach major professional firms to discuss their terms and fees. The first hour's discussion will be free, or it should be, and an immediate indication of the professionals' experience of buy-outs will come from their assessment of the team and the venture. For this purpose they should have asked you to bring much information. From now on it must be clear what the terms are. These may differ widely between firms and even within firms, depending on personal inclination and work-load. Also, different jobs can have large fee variations. Thus a long-shot chance which the team alone supports is likely to attract higher payments at each stage than a well-financed venture with a willing vendor and every prospect of, say, continuing audit and tax business.

A typical procedure for a medium-sized buy-out, with a total likely consideration of around £1 million, will be for the professional adviser to assess rapidly how much charged time will be needed to get to the first offer. Assuming this is charged at £3000, the professional then demands an immediate commitment from the team of approximately £750, in return for which he will speculate £2250 of his own time. There is thus risk to both sides. Naturally, at such rates, the team will be doing most of the work while the profession provides expertise, direction and finish to the business plan. There is always the option of the team doing less work in return for paying higher fees; such points are open to discussion.

Once the first offer has been made, it soon becomes possible to take a much better view on the final shape of the deal and the chances of completion. If the chances start to fall, the professional may be instrumental in winding down the approach rather than risk further time. Alternatively a higher proportion of fees paid to time spent may be demanded to continue negotiations. But more frequently, a view will be taken on when to approach the vendor to underwrite the professional fees. This has the useful advantage of establishing the vendor's commitment. In the event of completion, the fees are added to the price and so will fall mostly on the financing institutions. Thus in a successful buy-out or in a near miss, the team will pay little or nothing for professional advice. In situations such as contested bids this is not possible and inevitably one set of advisers and team members will be disappointed, but any team which actually pays fees on a pro rata basis from personal finances after a failed buy-out has not used enough foresight.

Some teams, having heard that 'the financiers somehow pay the professional fees in the end', decide to approach the financiers directly. Financiers can therefore be approached by teams with ventures which may or may not be viable, and which have not yet received any professional advice, asking for an indication of finance and a commitment on fees. The advisability of this course must remain an open question. Suffice to say that at the outset the financier does not know whether he will want to be the lead financier, the team does not know whether his will be the best offer and generally both sides need the option to drop the other party. Curiously, a detail such as professional fees seems out of place in such circumstances.

Aside from fees, perhaps the most important aspect

of looking for advisers is to find people whose personal qualities and style of business happen to suit the team. Most teams can expect to work for a long time, under pressure, in association with their advisers. There may be disappointments before the final success and under such conditions it is essential that there is personal rapport.

Producing the business plan

Since it will involve much time and trouble, the construction of the business plan may be left until the buy-out team has at least some indication of success. It can even be left until after the initial offer, though by this stage there is a risk of pressure of events. On the other hand, if there is time, ability and enthusiasm, there are advantages in completing a first draft of a provisional plan before looking for professional advice, particularly if there has been difficulty obtaining an indication of finance when a complicated deal is involved.

With establishing credibility for the buy-out team a prime purpose ahead of completion, much of the planning process may at first sight seem superfluous. In essence the plan is providing a basis for the future management and direction of the company. It requires thought, which in turn provokes more thought on forecasts, inter-related activities and their co-ordination. It is a process which most teams will not have experienced and so will introduce professional management methods to many organisations where few existed. It will indicate what the teams are good at doing and, by inference to an outsider, may show where some of the team's deficiencies lie. It is thus a prime instrument for the assessment of the team and will provide much information to prospective banks for this and other purposes. The needs of these functions should influence the form of the plan and in particular its length, which should not be so long that much of it is overlooked by its likely readers.

The plan may start with a descriptive background to the current position stating how the business started and developed, the activities in which it is involved, its suppliers and markets and its size. The financial position and tax history should be attempted, and the detail may even include the more important assets and their values. Explain why a buy-out has become the best option for ownership and control and describe the backgrounds of the buy-out team, giving extensive personal detail.

The planning process for events hereafter closely follows the procedure covered in the chapter on the divesting corporation. A mission and objectives are set, the strategy and policies are deduced which will achieve the mission, and then various forecasts and budgets are developed from the policies. By this time numerous inconsistencies may have become apparent and so the plan is adapted until it presents a feasible set of intentions. The difference involved in a forward plan in a buy-out is that with so many more uncertainties, the overall horizon of the plan is nearer than the five years or so for a mature corporation. In practice, indeed, there may be little point in extending it beyond three years, except possibly to show the cash flow implications of capital repayments.

Even three years is much longer than the effective time horizon nearly all teams will be working to in the first six months of independence. Adjusting to new positions of authority, sorting out the unexpected, the initial gearing and the dominant importance of cash flow are just some of the factors which require a disproportionate concern during the first three months. In effect the planning horizon is shortened for a temporary phase, and it recedes as the opening clutter of events are worked through, giving way once again to circumstances in which it is possible to take a longer view. By the end of the first year numerous variances and misconceptions are likely to have been revealed in the original plan from which subsequent plans may benefit greatly. Thus while some planning issues may seem elaborate for immediate purposes their full value will come through later.

Having set the direction which the business is to take, the implied master budget for perhaps two years is outlined. This consolidates numerous subsidiary budgets and will help to indicate inconsistencies between them. Several of these, such as production, personnel, marketing and sales should be outlined, so that from their contents it will be possible to start to construct a provisional cash flow budget, a profit and loss account and a subsequent balance sheet. Both expenses and working capital are usually under-estimated, so the team should aim to make adequate provision for these items. As the cash flow budget nears completion it will become possible to estimate more accurately financing needs and in turn to assess the financing charge.

At this stage of the first draft, and possibly before, it is valuable to isolate and list every forecast and assumption which has been made. Few of these will actually appear as forecasts, but rather as unstated assumptions and projections. Whenever there is a budget there is at least one or more underlying forecast, and the list of these will be long in even a small organisation. The aim should be to substantiate all of them, possibly improve them and then, using the assembled information, to build up narratives on topics such as production, administration and working capital. Since the sales forecast is crucial to nearly every other figure in the plan, there should be a particularly strong performance on marketing.

Finally, a number of general matters may be included in the first draft: proposed directors' con-tracts, insurance arrangements, redundancy costs and their provision, and the impact on the business of points of tax and law, many of which are covered elsewhere in this book. All are details which may be important and affect the buy-out or the competent running of the company.

A plan to this level of complexity should lie within the capabilities of every buy-out team. When it is presented to a professional adviser, criticism of its structure, content and forecasts should be expected and improvements may be suggested to the various schedules and projections, drawing attention to figures which will interest the financiers. The adviser will also be able to contribute a far better outline financing plan and provisional approach to the debt repayment. The latter could involve cash flow schedules for the next five years or so and if, as is often the case, these go beyond the limits of forecasting accuracy or procedure, they should merely be presented as illustrating the repayment of the debt, having no other implications.

With the plan at an advanced stage, a separate exercise, which typically justifies coverage in the plan itself, is a sensitivity analysis with the more important variables. This shows how cash flow, profits, debt-servicing capacity and so on are affected by changes in turnover, raw material prices, interest rates, wage costs or whatever the key variables happen to be. The procedure is greatly assisted by the use of a computerised spreadsheet, several types of which are widely available. This has the advantage that, once the model of the business is established, it can also be used to show rapidly the effects of points which arise during the negotiations, and of changing variables after the buy-out when the team are actually running the business. For the moment, however, perhaps the greatest value of a sensitivity analysis is in indicating the circumstances under which the business would become marginally viable. Many financiers working through plans immediately scale down many of the extragavant hopes, and in light of this the team's own forecasts may gain credibility from a comparison with results projected on unfavourable assumptions.

A criticism of spreadsheets is that a plan stands or falls by the information, linkages between activities and the many forecasts which it contains. Computerised methods have nothing to do with these factors; they merely work out their implications. Having fed in some assumptions and a data base, the figures flow with such ease as to give the impression that it is all going to happen, that the risks are minimised by virtue of using a computer. Management action or inaction are ignored when in practice they are the most important part of a buy-out and its consequences. But this is a minor criticism.

If he has not by this time persuaded the team to give up the idea of a buy-out the professional adviser will proceed to work on the proposed scheme and its tax implications in order to establish as far as possible the feasibility of the plan. This will finally clear the way for a second approach to the financiers in an attempt to get a firm assurance of finance ahead of the initial offer. Finance is not absolutely certain until just before completion, but the team will have an advantage during negotiations if it is virtually certain over a wide price range for the business. Furthermore, it may now be clear that the financier who gave the initial indication of finance is not the most suitable for the scheme and style of businesss in hand. If an alternative lead financier has to be found, now will clearly be the best time to look. Once the lead financier has started to work in depth on the proposal, any technical objections to the buy-out team, the business, its valuation and to the scheme may be expected to appear. This is the second most important category of reason for abandoning buy-outs after significant screening has started, the most important being the unwilling vendors already mentioned. Again, it is preferable to have this information as soon as possible.

The initial offer

The issue may be raised at the approach to the initial offer as to who will be involved in the negotiations. More than half the buy-out teams conduct the negotiations themselves with professional advice solely in a supporting role. Several financiers endorse this by taking the view that the team is the best judge of its own interests and will be demonstrating some relevant business acumen in prosecuting the proceedings to a successful conclusion. It is possible at times to discern just a hint of commercial machismo over who does what in the negotiations: either the team stands on its own feet or it is not worth supporting. There is, however, a complete range of opinion among financiers on the subject. Some financiers never participate on behalf of the buy-out team; others will participate if asked, but expect not to be asked; a few expect to participate unless asked not to, while a small minority insist on involvement. In all, between one third and 40 per cent of negotiations appear to involve major assistance of this nature, with less than 10 per cent of teams taking a secondary position to their advisers and financiers.

The argument for using a third party in the negotiations is that negotiating a financial deal over several months entails several skills which the team is unlikely to have acquired and a professional might therefore expect to get a better price. In addition, the team is in an inherently weaker negotiating position than the vendor from several standpoints and the neutral status of an outsider may help to overcome some of these. His involvement may indeed be seen as just one among several measures to strengthen the bargaining position of the team, a process which started soon after the first idea for the buy-out.

Having decided who is to negotiate, the initial offer is drawn up and sent to the vendor's decision-taker, who is normally the chief executive. The offer is usually a letter which in its simplest form will contain, subject to contract, what is being offered, for how much and when the first meeting will be. The object is to bring the vendor and the team into direct negotiations and, where there is doubt over the vendor's attitude, the offer should build up the team's standing with a price which is not too far out of line with reality.

Matters to be dealt with during the negotiations

The opening phase of the negotiations is to secure an agreement in principle. (Among several excellent checklists given in L. Blackstone and D. Franks (1984) is one on negotiating procedure for the buy-out team.) Once an agreement is attained on the concept of the buy-out, its probable scheme and likely price, the way is then clear to work on several time-consuming matters, thus:

The scheme of the buy-out and its financing

The final details of the scheme and the shape of the financing package will now be emerging. With so much prepared in advance of the negotiations and a willing vendor, little further work may be needed.

Tax planning implications of the buy-out scheme

The buy-out scheme will have been chosen primarily for the tax planning implications which must now be put into effect. Some require a certain sequence of events and at least an indication of approval from the Inland Revenue. Other necessary clearances will involve completion details of the buy-out, stock valuation, assets valuation and share valuation where this applies. Clearances will take a minimum of thirty days and possibly very much longer, though it is doubtful whether inordinate delay often occurs with proposals which involve a true and fair view and are carried out for bona fide commercial reasons. Having an adviser with an excellent working relationship with the Inland Revenue can greatly speed the process.

Buy-out team members' equity shares

Though small in relation to other sources of finance in most buy-outs, equity shares will be very important to the team members and in many cases the consequent financial arrangements will need time.

Class 4 transactions

These arise where the vendor is a public company and a team member is, or has been, a director of the company, or any of its subsidiaries. Clearance is then required from the Quotations Department of the Stock Exchange and typically is given against a certificate from the company's auditors that the proposed transaction is fair value. Where clearance is not given, a circular has to be sent to shareholders to obtain approval for the transaction.

Relations with customers

Obviously the customer base must be preserved and particular care will be needed where the trading relationships with other subsidiaries of the vendor form a major part of sales. A carefully timed public relations exercise may be required, though there should be little difficulty once it has been established that the new venture is a stable going concern.

Relations with suppliers

The assurance of continued support from creditors may be a major factor in the financier's decision to finance the buy-out. As a result, it may be necessary to inform suppliers of the new arrangements before informing customers.

Sustaining the negotiations

The complexity of most buy-outs bears little relation to the size of the overall transaction, and frequently the vendor is put to much trouble over a matter of almost insignificant proportion compared to other activities. With the final outcome in the balance right to the end, it can be important to maintain the vendor's interest in the transaction and to make at least some preparation for the threats which can arise. Over a long negotiating period, these will principally arise from an alternative divestment method or a counter offer, and some unobtrusive preparation for such a contingency may be in order. L. Blackstone and D. Franks (1984) have referred to the management walk-out, or the threat of it, as a possible counter in a difficult situation. D. Michaels (1983) has pointed out that in most cases, both negotiating parties will wish to avoid an un-resolved dispute and he has also referred to the value of the buy-out team allying itself with the workforce. Any possible advantages of this nature should be carefully considered.

The buy-out team will have prepared from an early stage for personal opposition and jealousy from other members of the vendor's staff. The value of this preparation will have increased as a conclusion becomes more certain, but whatever measures have been taken it is essential to move quickly towards completion once there is provisional agreement on price and terms. Another reason for speed is that the financiers and their legal advisers will have been introduced to the proceedings by this time, as too will the vendor's solicitor. Consequently there is a danger that matters may fall entirely into professional hands, some of whom will be under less pressure of time than the buy-out team. This final phase of negotiations may be greatly simplified and speeded if all the financiers use the same firm of solicitors.

5 Financing a buy-out

The procedure for financing was introduced in the previous chapter. Once a provisional plan covering the major features of the proposed venture has been drawn up, outlining how much finance appears to be needed, perhaps three financiers are approached for an initial indication of whether they will provide finance. After receiving an assurance, much more work is done on the business plan before the financiers are approached again. This time they will decide whether to commit extensive time and trouble to the application, so clearing the way for negotiations to begin with the vendor. The financier screens the venture, proposes the financing plan and syndicates the deal if necessary. When agreement in principle is reached with the vendor, the financier is able to participate in the final negotiations leading to completion.

Some differences between buy-outs and other banking business

Buy-outs differ in several ways from, for example, commercial lending for development to a medium-sized business. The structure of the deals can become elaborate and the negotiations protracted and complicated. Risks, returns and the general challenge of the proceedings all contrast with other areas of banking and require specialised skills and experience. Not surprisingly, the personalities attracted to it actually thrive on the conditions, several stressing the job interest, the fun, the sense of involvement and in all, the non-monetary attractions of their posts. Not surprisingly too, with most of the business new to the financing houses concerned, it is not difficult to detect entrepreneurial characteristics among some of the financiers themselves, an interesting contrast with, for example, the branch manager of the clearing bank (that is, one of the main high street banks) who has been the major banking contact before the buy-out for nearly all team members.

Another difference between buy-outs and routine commercial lending concerns the assessment of the business and the expectations of the financier. In commercial lending, the crucial point is whether or not the firm will survive and be able to service the debt. If it will, subsequent profits are something of an irrelevance except insofar as they provide cover, a safety margin for the bank. In the case a buy-out involving, as nearly all do, an equity stake the survival issue is only one factor. More important for many financing houses is the growth of profits and the ease and speed with which the investment can ultimately be realised. Naturally there are differences in emphasis on this point between financiers. Some put in a balanced quantity of equity and debt taking the view that they need a diversified portfolio for the longer term. Others place a strong emphasis on equity investment only, with an increased orientation towards the rapid elimination of debt, business performance and the inclusion of incentives for the buy-out team. As a result certain financiers are more suited to certain buy-outs and their teams. Details in schemes for the same buy-out can differ, as too can financing plans, simply as a result of applying to a different bank. These differences can be important and justify seeking an independent view on the financing plan.

At the time of writing, it is not difficult to finance a buy-out. Competition among the financiers is such that if a choice of provisional offers is not obtained with ease, there must be something seriously wrong with the proposal. However it would be rash to assume that these conditions will persist for long and when change does come in the banking world it tends to be rapid and initially imperceptible to outsiders. An economic downturn leading to a sudden rise in failures would lead many financiers to reconsider the market. Several have already predicted a shake-out among the peripheral financing institutions in view of the way they have been out-bid on some deals.

Fashionable though buy-outs may be, the competition among financiers is perhaps surprising as with most of the money made on capital appreciation over a period of years. Fully successful participation in the business requires a decision to run a portfolio of small to medium-sized investments, the majority of which are likely to remain unquoted. This is a specialised field of investment in which there are much greater difficulties over monitoring the holdings, even after expertise has been built up, compared with nearly all other investment fields. But many have overcome the problem and have decided to participate in this business. Here the attractions of buy-outs are clear: a rare opportunity to build up a worthwhile holding in an unquoted company; far less risk than new start-ups, since management and the business are largely proven and over the hurdle of learning to manage managers; and in the case of successes, the timescale to achieve a public quote tends to be much shorter than with a totally new venture.

Some unconventional sources of finance for buy-outs

Although a majority of buy-outs are handled by the specialist financiers, it is not absolutely essential to use them. Deals can be concluded using personal wealth, a simple clearing bank overdraft, leasing and even debt factoring. Where potential finance exists through some less formal means, but not enough to complete the deal, it may be possible to modify the financial plan using the source in an advantageous way. A disadvantage of some of these sources in the early stages is their unpredictability, both in amount and timing. This is the biggest current criticism made of numerous public sector grants for a variety of purposes; it is not known if they are coming or when, though some of the regional development agencies are reported as having a good record on clarity and speed of decision.

Possible forms of finance from the vendor are also uncertain. These can take the form of deferred payment, securing inter-company loans, residual equity stakes and leased assets, particularly where there are tax complications. The list is long, but there can be few who can anticipate such a source ahead of the negotiations. Rather, possibilities may emerge as points during negotiation after an initial assurance of finance from elsewhere has justified the opening offer.

The initial indication of finance

Most buy-out teams will be approaching the financiers in the hope that they will supply most of the finance. In the end, the financing plan may include major contributions from other sources but for the moment these will be speculative at best. For the initial indication of finance, attention will centre on the provisional price, the asset value, the profits, the outlook and the likelihood of any complications, notably with tax. Later, when the business plan is more thorough, it will be appropriate to consider at least three more questions.

- Can significant assets be sold soon after the buy-out?
- Is the business light on assets but employing valuable personnel so that there will be significant goodwill in the price to be paid?
- Is voting control for the buy-out team easily attainable, unlikely ever to be reached, or in the balance?

The first question affects the initial distortion to the gearing with a direct effect on the price which can be paid; it is unlikely to affect the choice of the financier. Whether there is likely to be goodwill in the price is highly important as in this case the venture will be much more difficult to finance. The question of voting control can also affect financing if control is in the balance. However, at an early stage, it may not be possible to take a view on this unless the result is a foregone conclusion, depending as it will on details of price and personal finances which may be far from clear until well into the negotiations. Both these latter questions can affect the choice of financier. The lead financier can be changed, but with the buy-out team attempting to build up credibility and the outside danger of the venture gaining the status of unwanted property on the financing circuit, it is greatly preferable to choose correctly the first time.

Screening the business

The financier is likely to have been approached for an initial financing indication; the team is likely to have returned later with much more information; gradually the deal takes shape. Eventually the financier realises he is the lead financier and more time is justified on the application. Much of the screening involves the assessment of the team and this must be anticipated at its formation as was indicated in the previous chapter. The assessment of the business is not necessarily a separate issue, but it will first be screened by the financier and then subsequently by technical consultants and reporting accountants. Often, these reports will be made available to the team and they may introduce a note of caution. After all, recent results will hardly have been outstanding. The investigations will rely heavily on historic information and little or no allowance may be made for those entrepreneurial qualities which have yet to be introduced to affect the picture. Nonetheless, these reports may be expected to provide an excellent basis for a reappraisal of the whole venture.

Putting the deal together

Here, a flexible approach must be expected. With the scheme of the buy-out liable to revision, all major factors differing from one buy-out to another and important variables changing right up to completion, several financiers have stressed the need for a totally creative treatment.

Partly as a result, the features of deals which receive widespread attention after the event, the gearing against profits and the equity proportion within the whole consideration, tend to be treated as secondary factors by the financiers. Rather than saying that the interest cover shall be, for example, twice, the deal is first structured, the cover then checked and so long as it is broadly within a target range, it is of little further consequence. Many, indeed, claim to disregard gearing altogether. It is often difficult to work out the implied gearing for a complicated capital structure, the result can be misleading if there are to be asset sales and in any case you have to look for a year beyond completion for some meaningful income figures. Besides, most of the questions raised by gearing which concern profits, capital structure and debt servicing are all asked independently.

Capital structure and mezzanine finance

Traditionally a company will have some equity and some debt, and the ratios between the two will principally determine the strength of the balance sheet. The debt will be split between long and short term debt and the interest rates thereon may be fixed or floating. With buy-outs, however, there is usually little equity available.

Many financiers actually want to see that the buy-out team has voting control and the incentive which goes with it, but the limitations of personal finance typically constrain the proportion of equity available to the team with a conventional capital structure. The solution is either to reduce the size of the equity and compensate the higher risk on the debt with a greater return, or else to secure the debt on the assets, give it a normal return and create a category of capital known in the US as mezzanine finance.

Mezzanine finance can take a variety of forms. For example, it may be unsecured debt with a much higher yield and some separate equity participation right such as a medium-term option or warrant. The disadvantage of this approach is that debt-service from gross profits may start to jeopardise the value of the company in the event of a flotation, while fixed participation rights will inevitably dilute the equity, albeit with a delay. Consequently there is widespread popularity in the UK for using convertible, redeemable preference shares as the mezzanine capital. They are serviced out of net profits, so providing the financiers with the advantage of taxed or franked income and may have their terms varied to suit all parties to the deal. If the company goes very well, everyone concerned will want to see the preference shares redeemed so that the market value of the company is enhanced. On the other hand, if a poor trading performance means that the preference dividend is an unacceptable burden on cash flow, its conversion to equity, with dilution of the buy-out team's proportion, will be the best solution. Between those two positions there is room for a variety of management incentives.

Working capital and the buy-out

The position of working capital is frequently complicated by a long-standing relationship between the business and its clearing bank, who hitherto may have been the sole source of external finance. Apart from the aims and objectives of the buy-out financier being distinctly different to those of the clearer, who may view with dismay the upheaval of an old customer, there is the problem of providing adequate finance for working capital through a period when needs will be volatile. It is suggested that as much working capital as possible is funded. If US practice is followed, the financing plan will include what Americans term an 'evergreen portion', that is, finance secured on the working capital with no fixed repayment schedule, but full flexibility over redemption.

The buy-out team's equity contribution and collateral

The buy-out team may provide only a small proportion

of the total finance, but in nearly every case, it will be far and away their largest personal portfolio investment. There appear to be few rules over just how much they should provide except that the financiers will want to see them committed to a severe loss, in relation to their personal worth, in the event of a failure. Having required so much personal risk and commitment, no additional formal collateral is needed by the financiers.

In practice, however, further exposure is widespread. It arises from the clearing banks who provide the overdraft and day-to-day banking services and from the difficulties which arise when the vendor refuses to give certain warranties. The clearing banks are on the sidelines of the negotiations and usually give continuity of service to the new company, but personal guarantees can be required. Warranties may simply fall on the buy-out team personally and it is then up to them to try to establish liability on the part of their professional advisers. As a result, in many cases, a failure can place a much heavier strain on the team than the mere loss of their equity.

Insurance of the buy-out team

The importance of the team to the success of the venture and to everyone concerned is such that substantial life insurance cover will be strongly considered.

Refinancing the buy-out

There are many reasons why most buy-outs will consider refinancing within five years of completion, and some will wish to review the possibility when the financing plan is assembled. Recently, nearly all the refinancing has reflected and built upon success. Funds are needed for expansion as a result of growth;

teams want the greater financial flexibility following the elimination of the initial gearing; substantial capital growth leads to members and institutions wanting to lighten holdings and diversify portfolios; all these and more are symptomatic of progress and success. Some buy-outs will need to be refinanced for other reasons, in particular the companies which are not going to fail but cannot raise cash flow sufficiently to service and repay debt. For these the opportunities will be more restricted. Moratoria of debt repayments may be available as a last resort, but other forms of refinancing from the original sources are unlikely and attention will turn to the alternatives. Two of these are now considered.

The Business Expansion Scheme

This is a government scheme under which private individuals receive tax relief at their highest marginal rates, up to 60 per cent in the current tax year, against portfolio equity investments approved for the purpose. Started in 1983, the scheme superseded the Business Start-up Scheme which, by limiting investments to start-ups only, proved to have very limited application. In addition to start-ups, the Business Expansion Scheme is intended to promote and develop small to medium-sized companies and some of its restrictions are an attempt to achieve this purpose. Thus although the idea of buy-outs is in line with the spirit of the scheme, aid from the latter cannot be used for the purchase of shares, so restricting Inland Revenue clearance to asset deals. However, it is arguable that the scheme would always be very much a minor source even without this limitation, as there is no shortage of takers for the equity in a buy-out prior to completion.

After the buy-out, the Business Expansion Scheme becomes much more easy to apply. The various restrictions, problems of clearance and problems of investment appraisal mean that nearly all individuals have to work through an approved fund. In turn this creates sources of substantial funds for the medium-sized business. The finance must be through the equity, but this is no drawback if, for example, a team member wants to leave and sell out, or if the alternative is to face the conversion terms on another class of capital. The overall cost and implications of raising money from such a fund might usefully be compared with the expense of development finance from other sources.

Coming to the market

Perhaps the most important source of funds for buy-outs in their early years will be the equity market. Coming to the market has other attractions too. The money motive may be well down the entrepreneur's list of priorities but that is not to say it is off the list altogether. Until a quote is obtained, the full implications of the substantial personal capital created by the buy-out team are most unlikely to be apparent. On the day of its flotation, the buy-out has finally arrived.

Why not come to the market as soon as possible after completion? Initially there is likely to be a lacklustre balance sheet with a background of mundane matters to attend to. Thus on the grounds of pressure of events, all but a few exceptions will leave such a move until after the second year, though the intention can be part of the planning process very early on. Initially too, it is valid to raise the more general objection that a quote places greater exposure on a company and its management. Information which was just about 'publicly-available', now becomes widely disseminated; there is pressure for final results, for interim results and in various ways this can be to the detriment of the longer view. Many will not be ready for such conditions for a couple of years. Finally, some tax advantages outlined in Chapters 6 and 7 may be lost with a full quote relative to a private company and specialist advice should be taken both on the current position and on whether, as with the Venture Capital Scheme, the unlisted markets are exempt from the definition of 'full quote'.

Making a market in the shares of the smaller company is now much simpler and less costly than it was just a few years ago. Then it was either necessary to obtain a full market quote, with its regulations and expense, or to consider the over the counter markets and dealings under Stock Exchange Rule 163(2). Under this rule bargains are only possible when both buyer and seller are matched in terms of the number of shares on offer, a limitation which affects marketability and the speed of transactions, so precluding many of the purposes for which a company may be coming to the market. If a company's needs are limited, and likely to remain so, such a share market has the advantages of few regulations, low costs and little publicity, but most companies will want a wider market before long.

There are several regulations to be complied with for a full quote of which perhaps the most important is that at least 25 per cent of the equity must be made available to the public. Regulations on advertising also increase the cost of the issue. These difficulties have largely been overcome since 1980 by the Unlisted Securities Market (USM). Here, the minimum equity to be publicly held is only 10 per cent and other regulations reduce the issue costs substantially. Expenses depend very much on the method of issue. From an analysis of actual smaller issues with a market capitalisation between £10 and £12 million, County Bank have supplied the following figures:

USM Flotation method

	Introduction	Placing	Offer for sale
£'000	105	150	300

Source: County Bank (1984)

By comparison a full listing offer for sale will cost between £360000 and £500000, and typically nearer the upper figure. However, a direct comparison may be misleading due to the greater complication of many of the companies choosing a full listing, with higher fees for accountants and lawyers as a result.

A market introduction involves arranging a quote without issuing more shares, so that for those raising capital the choice is between a placing, that is an offer to known investors, and an offer for sale, which involves advertising to a wider market. The disadvantage of a placing is that it is unlikely to achieve such a broadly-based share register as an advertised offer. This breadth is valuable later on if further capital has to be raised, or if substantial lines of stock are to be moved at short notice. Another criticism of placings is that they can lead to a potential conflict of interest between the vendor, the issuing broker and his clients, though this danger can be minimised by using a merchant bank for the issue.

To a large extent, a choice between methods is dictated by the amount to be raised. The Stock Exchange limit the amount to be raised by a placing to £3 million provided that the overall market capitalisation does not exceed £15 million. For the raising of amounts above £3 million, the merits of an offer for sale would probably have made it the clear choice anyway. Expense will be a major argument against full quotes unless more than £7 million is to be raised, but the issue is principally decided by the size of the company. A large company can benefit greatly from the attention and publicity involved in obtaining a full quote[1].

---

[1] The author is grateful to Mr S. Metcalf of County Bank for supplying much of the information on coming to the market.

6

Organising the new company: some tax and law

Most of the tax and law in this book has been divided between two chapters of which this is the first. The coverage provided is not comprehensive and notably excludes much company secretarial information, but rather it is orientated towards some of the choices which may be made during the early stages when professional help may not be available. Much of the material has implications for tax planning and tax avoidance and there may be dismay at the prospect of having to use procedures and ideas which run counter to some of the more constructive entrepreneurial instincts. Indeed many entrepreneurs may view tax avoidance with a certain mild cynicism, having their attention firmly on maximising after-tax income, rather than minimising the tax to be paid. Accordingly, it is important to distinguish between avoidance methods using contrived schemes and measures involving planning and Inland Revenue clearance in order to smooth the path of bona fide commercial transactions. There is no easy division between the two, but where the implications of a buy-out plan are assessed and the most tax-efficient path chosen, the measures may be expected to fall into the latter category.

Why not organise as a public limited company?

Virtually all buy-outs are organised initially as private limited companies. Later on, many obtain a public quote and some of the compelling reasons for doing so are outlined in the chapter on financing the buy-out. However, none of the public company advantages apply before a buy-out. In addition the provisions of Section 43 of the Companies Act 1981 apply only to private companies, thereby seriously limiting the choice of buy-out schemes available if the company to be bought out has a quote.

Why not organise as a sole trader or partnership?

Some purchases of small firms and partnership succession transactions carried out by unincorporated businesses have the characteristics of buy-outs. These purchases are relatively small, inconspicuous and financed through less formal, private sources of finance. Among deals handled by the main buy-out financiers there are only one or two examples of a partnership.

At first sight this may seem surprising. The traditional banker's objection, that a floating charge cannot be taken on the business assets alone, may be overcome to a large extent through leasing and the creation of limited partnerships for the financiers. The unincorporated form can have many advantages which will depend on the situation, such as the avoidance of close company legislation, the ease with which capital can be withdrawn from the business and the tax advantages at the time of starting.

There are several tax advantages for unincorporated businesses. Buy-out teams will be particularly interested by the recovery of schedule E taxation which they have paid during the three years prior to the start up. This relief is available against the expenses involved in preparing for the venture over a three year period before starting and against assessed trading losses during the first four years of trading. Though trivial in relation to the total cost of a buy-out, the sums are nonetheless large compared with most team members' capital investment in the venture. That this allowance is unclaimed because buy-outs are not normally organised as partnerships may be explained partly by the considerable trouble and risk to which financiers would be put merely for the benefit of the team members. However it may also be explained by a broader historical view of unincorporated businesses. They have proved unsuitable for large operations with a large capital base.

Why not organise as a co-operative?

Forming a co-operative under the Industrial and Provident Society Acts 1965 and 1976 creates an organisation with legal properties similar to a private limited company run by directors who are also shareholders. There is a limitation on financial liability to the capital investment; the organisation is a separate legal entity; there is no joint and several liability for the directors beyond negligence and the obligation to fulfil the call of duty and information. Like companies too, returns are required which must be produced to a certain standard. There is a difference regarding the minimum number of members: two for a company, seven for a co-operative. Also anomalies can arise over minor pieces of legislation in which it seems the co-operatives have been overlooked. For example the tax rate for co-operatives, normally identical to the small company rate, has recently been out of line. There can also be differences which arise from the rules adopted by co-operatives at their registration, but identical provisions can be adopted with a company's Articles and Memorandum. If a co-operative's rules were drawn up so as to avoid, for example, the close company legislation, it is doubtful whether they would be accepted.

Despite the similarities with companies, Industrial and Provident Society co-operatives have been an unsuccessful form of organisation for buy-outs so far. Of the buy-outs handled by the financiers interviewed, less than one per cent have involved a co-operative. Some co-operatives have been handled by the various public-sector agencies which have organised a few buy-outs. Had these been interviewed the total might have risen to perhaps one and a half per cent. It would also have risen had co-operatives organised as companies been included with, for example, an employee share trust, but this begs the issue; nearly all buy-outs are achieved with a limited company as the vehicle.

Opinions on co-operatives differed widely among the financiers interviewed; several were open to approaches from them. Doubts were expressed as to whether the organisation adopted by many co-operatives is really suited to the rigours of a buy-out, but this has little to do with the form of the business. If a fifteen-head buy-out team, with a committee structure for all management matters and decisions taken by equal votes, was to propose a buy-out, they would face similarly long odds against success. The form of their organisation, whether company or co-operative, would be irrelevant. As a result, if a co-operative structure is proposed there are perhaps three points to work on during preparation: firstly to ensure there will be competent, credible, professional management;

secondly, to avoid any ultimate succession problem which will oblige outsiders to raise substantial sums to buy themselves in; and thirdly, to provide the financiers with an appropriate return which can be realised as easily as selling shares in a company. These ends must be achieved through the rules adopted by the co-operative, a measure which may delay registration*.

Close companies

Alternatives may be considered by buy-out teams, but most will be working out the implications of incorporation. Prominent among these will be the close company legislation. The definition of a close company can be complex, but essentially for a private company it is one which is controlled by five or fewer shareholders or by its directors, irrespective of their number. The term 'directors' here includes associates such as relatives and trustees of related settlements. The definition is less restrictive for quoted companies where the public has at least 35 per cent of the voting equity and the five largest members have no more than 85 per cent of the votes. This may be a reason for incorporation but at the outset many, indeed possibly the majority, of companies contemplated by buy-out teams are likely to be close companies.

Directors' expenses within close companies

One consequence of being a close company is the slightly sharper focus of attention on certain expenses to directors. If these are not wholly and necessary for the business, they can be treated as a distribution, rather than as earned income and so possibly attract a

---

* Further information is available from the Co-operative Development Agency, 20 Albert Embankment, London SE1 7TJ.

higher rate of tax and an advance corporation tax penalty where relief is not yet available, though the former is only a remote possibility after the ending of the investment income surcharge. However, it is doubtful whether any expenses will actually be paid unless they are wholly and necessary for the business.

Apportionment of the profits of a close company

Perhaps the most important of the close company provisions are the measures to oppose the accumulation of capital in certain types of company. Where income is either classified as estate or investment income, as opposed to trading income, profits may be apportioned by the Inland Revenue among the members and treated as a distribution even if no dividend has been paid. Where apportionment is a danger, it may be opposed by showing that a dividend prejudices the requirements of a company's business. Such proof may be simple in the early years of independence when cash flow is clearly being used for expansion and the repayment of debt. It may also be simple later on in cases where high growth and extreme risk are inherent in the business. However, where there is an outside chance of future liability the buy-out team should take specialist advice and plan accordingly. The provisions are notoriously difficult to avoid directly; the aim should be to alter the shareholding so that the company falls outside the close company definition. This can take careful planning and time.

Tax relief on interest to buy shares

Recent legislation offers an advantage to close companies through Schedule E tax relief given against the interest on loans most buy-out teams will raise personally to purchase their equity. To qualify, the company must be a trading company and the individual must be at manager level or above, owning at least 5 per cent of the equity or spending over half his time on the management of the company.

Alternatively, the company need not be a close company to obtain this relief provided that the employees own 51 per cent of the equity. In this case there must be at least six employees and the company must be unquoted.

Share incentive and option schemes

Close company provisions introduce complications partly since they are intended to be anti-tax avoidance legislation. Measures taken in the early 1970s to combat executive share options also introduce a pitfall for buy-outs. Incentive and option schemes can take various forms and the opposing legislation has to have a comparably broad scope. This is a source of difficulty. The problem arises if shareholder directors can be considered as having established a share incentive scheme for themselves over a seven year period from the original share purchase, something which can occur if the share purchase is at the same time as the buy-out completion. The solution for a simple, uncomplicated situation is to acquire the shares significantly in advance of phasing in the actual business and its trade. But there are likely to be complications. Many buy-outs for example, will actually include share capital conversion provisions which are intended to provide management with an incentive and these must fall outside the scope of approved option schemes. As the legislation refers to identical treatment for shareholders within a share class, a solution can be to create different share classes with different rights. Specialist advice is essential here. The consequence of an unapproved share option is for the amount of any implied gain to be taxed as income. Payment of any tax is now allowed over five years.

Official attitudes towards approved share option schemes have softened under the current Tory administration. Save-as-you-earn option schemes with an upper limit of £50 per month were allowed from 1980 and this amount was doubled in 1984. However even at this level it is doubtful whether such a measure can have any effect on the financing of buy-outs. Legislation for a broader category of share incentive schemes without a savings component is expected, again with a size limitation, so that it is uncertain whether this measure too will ever lead to a buy-out.

The sale of shares and the disposal of the business

Ahead of a buy-out it may seem premature to think of matters very far in the future such as retirement. Besides there may be little point in compromising current interests when there is a probability of future changes in legislation. After all it is unlikely that anyone twenty years ago could usefully have antici-pated many subsequent tax measures. Capital gains tax had not been introduced. Corporation tax, capital transfer tax, taxation by the imputation system, value added tax, all had never even been heard of. Tax changes at only a quarter of this rate over the next twenty years could easily invalidate tax planning decisions today. This is the main argument against doing anything about capital gains tax and capital transfer tax at the time of the buy-out. If something is to be done, however, the planning may have to start early.

Capital gains tax

Aside from the reliefs available from the minimum threshold level, and from gifts which are really too small to allow substantial tax planning on the scale needed with buy-outs, capital gains tax may either be avoided through a share-for-share deal or through retirement relief. To qualify for the latter, the business must be a family company. This means you must either own at least 25 per cent of the equity, or 5 per cent if your family also control 51 per cent in all. Further, you must be a full-time working director and have owned the equity for ten years to obtain the full relief. If these conditions are met you qualify for relief on a tranch of assets for each year of your age above sixty, reaching the maximum allowed at sixty-five. At this stage, it is not actually necessary to retire.

Capital transfer tax

Substantial relief can be available, but once again the legislators have had the sole trader-cum-small family business in mind when drafting the provisions rather than the buy-out team. To qualify for business property relief, you must have a business which is not wholly or mainly in investments or property and have owned it for more than two years. If the shares to be transferred gave the transferor control of the company prior to the transfer, relief against capital transfer tax is then considerable. If you hold a minority shareholding instead of control, and the company is unquoted, relief is available at a reduced rate. This relief is lost if the company obtains a quote, a point which should cause some teams to reconsider a flotation and to check whether the Unlisted Securities Market is exempt for this purpose from the definition of public quote (see p. 73).

Directors' contracts and shareholders' agreements

Rather than thinking of how to sell out, the immediate concern after a buy-out is that a team member will actually leave at a time when he will be difficult to replace. Such a move could jeopardise the whole venture. Accordingly the directors' contracts and the wording of any restrictions on shareholders should be so organised as to help to hold the team together for an appropriate period.

The details of any clauses to this effect in the Articles of Association may be complicated and might include the required agreement of all members to any share transfer; first refusal on any share sale to rest with the other members; sale at a discounted price if a transfer is made within a specified time period, and so on. The aim should to be dissuade anyone from leaving, while making possible for a member to be removed if it should become necessary. As with the initial share purchase, care should be taken not to set up an unapproved incentive scheme.

The acquisition by the company of its own shares

Tax planning against a background of the extreme uncertainty of a buy-out and its aftermath have been greatly assisted by the provisions of Sections 45-62 of the Companies Act 1981, which allow a company to purchase its own shares. Sales of equity by departing team members and institutional investors can now be handled so that control is retained by the survivors, without necessarily having to raise personal finance. For the share vendor it can mean the difference between a sale and being locked in as a minority shareholder for the foreseeable future.

Though open to both private and public companies, the latter can only use distributable profits for this purpose, which could severely limit the scale of such redemptions. Private companies can also redeem shares out of capital, once distributable profits have been absorbed, raising fresh amounts if necessary for the purpose. If a large amount of equity is to be repurchased in the future, this additional facility could be another important argument against obtaining a quote.

The Venture Capital Scheme

It may be inappropriate to be thinking of failure before a buy-out, but for those who are not successful and lose some or all of their equity, relief is available against subsequent personal taxation under the Venture Capital Scheme. As relief is only available against losses on equity, the scheme's importance at an early stage of a buy-out lies in ensuring that all capital contributions are actually made through the equity, and that all purchases are of fresh, hitherto unissued shares. This latter point also applies after the buy-out if additional shares are offered. The deal should be arranged so that shares actually bought are fresh. While companies considering a flotation may be among the least likely to fail, the benefits of the venture capital scheme are lost if a full public quote is obtained.

7

Choosing a scheme for the buy-out: some other points of tax and law

Aside from the implications of incorporation, several points of law and most of the tax involved in a buy-out may relate to decisions over the scheme of the buy-out and its detail. The decisions are not straightforward since they can emerge throughout the negotiations up to completion. Choices are affected by the negotiations, yet unless there is some idea of the outcome right at the start, it is impossible to know how much to offer and for what, and whether financing is likely.

A decision on the buy-out scheme can be simple if it is only necessary to consider the interests of the team. Unfortunately this will rarely be the case, as on numerous points the interests of the vendor may be expected to be diametrically opposed. It is essential to appreciate and combine both sets of interests and when this is done many of the questions change. Rather than consider whether a point is favourable or unfavourable to either party, there is merely an implication for the price or a detail to be investigated.

Because of the need to view both parties' interests, most points of tax and law may be seen as adjuncts to the valuation process for the company. In this context, nearly all the resulting decisions have implications for one or all of three following questions:

- What price should be offered for a business?
- What price is the vendor likely to accept?
- What other complications are there, notably on tax?

These may help to place some complex issues in their appropriate perspective.

Although something of an aside from the decisions on a scheme, the issue of the accuracy of information will be raised as soon as an investigation starts. There are two sides to the problem: establishing from available records what the position is supposed to be and then ensuring that the records are complete and correct. There is room for argument over numerous valuations. The basis on which historic profits have been taken must be understood and the tax history in particular must cover all likely contingencies. All can and do have adverse consequences for the buyer. Indeed several cases of troubled buy-outs are reported where some historic tax issue has appeared after completion. Where this happens there will be the possibility of negligence claims against professional advisers or the vendor's auditors, but almost inevitably this will be a most unsatisfactory course of action. In a situation where substantial damages are sought, the immediate concern will be over the cash flow which has suffered, and the uncertain outcome of expensive and time-consuming civil action two or three years hence will be minor compensation. Besides, the buy-out teams are usually in the best position to analyse the records and in effect, will be assuming joint responsibility with their advisers on most matters.

Warranties and indemnities

However thorough an investigation, there will be areas of uncertainty on which the team will want a guarantee from the vendor. Moreover the financiers will normally insist on many of them. These are covered by warranties and indemnities. A warranty is a statement which asserts that certain details on the accounts, tax position or on other matters such as trademarks and contracts are indeed as indicated. These details are then warranted as correct by the vendor who is liable for damages if there is a breach of warranty. Indemnities, by contrast, have a more specific application, notably in connection with tax. If a certain liability arises the vendor directly compensates the buyer. Normally warranties and indemnities will apply for six years from the date they are given.

There are numerous limitations to warranties and indemnities. Their scope and application are often carefully drawn up. They are qualified with the statement 'to the best of knowledge, information and belief' and thus they will not necessarily point to a clear solution in a civil action. They are also notoriously difficult to obtain from the vendor so that where they are essential for financing, they can fall on the buy-out team themselves. As a result, the best approach ahead of the event is to analyse the buy-out thoroughly and use such adverse contingencies as exist to help obtain a lower purchase price, confining warranties and indemnities to matters which are mandatory for financing.

The purchase of assets as a buy-out scheme

A company is formed and buys assets from the parent;

this is usually by far the most simple scheme for a buy-out from the standpoint of the team. In the early years of buy-outs, over half the deals were completed by this method as it avoided Section 54 of the Companies Act 1948. Recently, however, the popularity of assets has fallen so that currently they are believed to form around one-fifth of deals, though the proportion varies between financiers, several of whom favour them. The introduction of the Business Expansion Scheme in 1983 provides another reason for buying assets, but it is more than offset by the announcement that initial investment allowances are to be phased out from 1984.

The disadvantages of such a scheme fall very much on the vendor. In buying assets, the buy-out team chooses just those items which are wanted, leaving behind superfluous items, current assets of contentious value, and potential liabilities from old contracts, taxation, or any other source. They will also leave behind all the employees and will be free to re-engage only as many as they want. Those who are re-engaged have no continuity of service, but must first be made redundant at the vendor's expense. In many cases, this could be the outstanding feature of asset deals for the team and the most costly objection for the vendor.

Capital allowances

The purchased assets will attract the capital allowances based on their cost, which can be offset against the taxable profit of the buyer. As already noted the initial allowances are being phased out. They have been reduced from 100 per cent to 75 per cent from March 1984 and will fall to 50 per cent after 1 April 1985 and to zero a year later. Writing-down allowances on the balance remain as before.

Initial allowances apply principally to plant and

machinery. Industrial buildings will not attract an initial allowance unless constructed and occupied from new and, naturally, all buildings will be second-hand in a buy-out. Instead they will attract writing-down allowances if they are less than fifty years old, which will be related to the qualifying expenditure and to their age. This is subtracted from a twenty-five year life for expenditure after 5 November 1962 and from a fifty year life for expenditure before that date. These allowances can be substantial, depending on the exact age of the building. There may be complications from other assets such as cars which have different allow-ances, but initially, at least, these can be ignored; the principle is that with the purchase of assets, substantial allowances will arise to be offset against taxable profit.

Stock relief clawback

Many of the problems left with the vendor depend precisely on what has been transferred. Historic stock relief, for example, can be clawed back if a trade or part of a trade has been transferred; but if there is only a partial transfer, the vendor merely retains the potential for future clawback. For certain sales the point at which clawback may or may not occur will depend on the judgement of the Inland Revenue and the team's tax adviser.

Development land tax

Development land tax also poses a problem; it is charged on a disposal, but not when a business is transferred from one company to another. At some stage, transferred assets may be considered as con-stituting a business and so establish avoidance. In other cases, there may be scope for avoidance by offsetting development land tax against a capital gains tax liability on the same asset.

Capital gains tax

Capital gains tax liability will arise for the vendor where there are capital gains on assets, unless it can be shown that a business was transferred as a going concern for shares or debentures. This can be difficult and in any case, a purchase for shares is usually unattractive. Avoidance measures should therefore concentrate on reducing the capital gains by allotting values to the various assets within reasonable limits, and then by offsetting any actual liability with roll-over relief. Sell a qualifying asset and purchase others either up to one year before, or three years after, the disposal and the base cost of the new asset will be adjusted for the capital gains tax liability. With new assets which fall rapidly in value, the tax is avoided altogether. For many organisations, capital gains tax need be no more than an administrative complication.

Balancing charges

Balancing charges are incurred when assets are sold for which initial investment allowances were given, but on which the annual writing-down allowances are not yet exhausted. If the disposal value is less than the qualifying expenditure, adjusted for age, there is a qualifying allowance instead. The latter is treated as a deduction from taxable profit, whereas balancing charges are additions. Calculation of these charges in the case of plant and machinery is by adjusting any disposal surplus or deficit with a notional 25 per cent pa straight-line writing-down allowance. Thus after two years only half the charge will be liable to tax and after four years it is waived altogether. Consequently, balancing charges are relatively simple to isolate for plant and machinery. In many cases, too, they will be negligible.

Much more difficult to isolate however are the balancing charges on industrial buildings. The procedure is similar to that for plant and machinery, but formidable complications can be introduced by adjusting the original capital expenditure for the land value, for certain aspects of subsequent maintenance, industrial building allowances and any previous balancing charges. Writing-down at 4 per cent pa for expenditure after 5 November 1962 and 2 per cent pa for prior expenditure up to fifty years, together with the necessary precision over dates, all contribute sufficient complication as to place the calculation beyond the scope of the casual observer. The final charges can be very large for certain items. Where this is the case, there may be justification for a separate leasing agreement on the assets, thereby leaving ownership unchanged.

The purchase of a company or subsidiary as a buy-out scheme

The majority of buy-outs currently involve the purchase of a company or subsidiary as the major feature of the scheme. Unlike assets purchases, assets transferred with a company do not confer capital allowances on the purchaser, except for the balance of any writing-down allowances which remain to be offset. Matters are greatly simplified for the vendor by a company sale as there is no stock relief clawback, development land tax, capital gains tax or assets or balancing charges to crystallise. In addition, all the attributes of a going concern are no longer the vendor's responsibility. Many of these have considerable value and both parties will want to ensure their correct assessment and to see that all contentious issues associated with them have been isolated. Matters for investigation could include contracts with suppliers and customers, trade agreements, patents, licences, tradenames, trademarks and so on. Above all perhaps, the workforce will be transferred.

If the implications seem a great burden on the buy-out team, it must be remembered that the balance of advantage can be assessed only in relation to the price of the deal and that frequently the vendor will sell a company while refusing to strip out some of the assets.

Personnel matters and industrial relations

Under current legislation, employees' rights and obligations continue through the transfer of ownership of a company so that employees' continuity of service is maintained. Liability for redundancy payments is also transferred and its size should be very carefully assessed. It is possible to lay off some of the workforce well ahead of the buy-out with redundancy payments falling on the vendor, but such a move can be expected to affect the price. Trade union agreements are also transferred, together with all union recognition. This can cause considerable difficulty if a small part of a larger organisation is transferred, together with several unions and elaborate demarcation, producing features which would not normally apply in a medium-sized business.

There is a statutory duty for both the vendor and purchaser to inform the trade union representatives of the impending change. There must be sufficient notice for consultation to take place amongst the affected parties. Any significant changes in duties, working conditions and general requirements of the labour force after transfer can support a claim for constructive dismissal, so the nature of any agreements, fringe benefits and renumeration details should be clearly established. A major source of difficulty can be pension rights. These are not legally transferred, but are open to negotiation and can be an important cause of obstruction from employees.

Tax losses

Unlike assets deals, tax losses are carried forward in a company sale for offset against subsequent taxable income. Although of substantial benefit to the purchaser and to the vendor, where it is not possible to offset them, tax losses may be easily overvalued. Frequently they provide no immediate benefit since there is no historic taxable profit. In such cases any future returns must be heavily discounted ahead of a buy-out. A further problem over tax losses arises from the tightening of avoidance legislation. In order to obtain the tax relief it is necessary to maintain the same trade for at three years subsequent to the change of ownership. The Inland Revenue has considerable discretion over the detail of what constitutes a change of trade and these powers could be used to discriminate against cases where activity is not entirely for bona fide commercial reasons.

Stock valuation

Stock valuation tends to be one of the more contentious points about buy-outs in general. It is also the subject of much negotiation since the vendor normally wants a high stock valuation with a correspondingly low figure on other assets, and vice versa for the purchaser. The Inland Revenue has an established practice for valuing the stock of a new company and clearance is required, so introducing a limit to actual distortions of value between stock and other assets. Nevertheless, it is appropriate to question whether a valuation is a true and fair view, or whether it is erroneous.

Stock reserve account

Buy-outs with a low stock valuation will appear to have abnormally high profits in the first year and so appear successful, albeit at the cost of a higher tax charge. In an interview one financier has suggested the creation of a stock reserve account in this situation, with apportionment of an abnormal gain to taxable profits over several years.

Share valuation

Arguably to a greater extent than stock, share valuation is open to conflicting opinions. Partly for this reason, clearance of a valuation with the Inland Revenue can be delayed, but partly also for other purposes such as a capital transfer tax assessment for which the clearance is also needed. The Inland Revenue aim for a 'just and reasonable' valuation based on information almost certainly inferior to that of the buy-out parties, so the limits of the discussion can be open to conjecture. The valuation affects stamp duty, a minor detail which may be avoided almost entirely, and capital gains tax. Avoidance of capital gains tax can be more difficult and may be assisted with an early view of the approximate valuation.

Capital gains tax

This tax does not arise where there is a share-for-share deal, but the purchaser will almost certainly object to the implied equity dilution even if the vendor prefers an unquoted share to cash. It is also possible to avoid capital gains tax if the purchase is made with distributable profits and this procedures offers much scope in buy-outs. Another method of avoidance is to deplete the company of assets on which the chargeable gains are arising and sell these separately, so attracting roll-over relief for the vendor. Roll-over relief is available on assets sales but not on shares. With careful planning, little or no capital gains tax need be paid.

Many buy-outs appear to be of companies whose value will represent a chargeable loss and some planning by the vendor may do much to ensure its rapid offset, after realisation, against available gains.

Hiving down

Many of the characteristics of asset and company purchases can be preserved by a process known as hiving down. This involves the creation of a new subsidiary into which the assets for sale are transferred. Personnel can also be transferred into the new subsidiary so giving the buyer choice over the size and composition of the labour force. Rights and benefits are the same for those chosen as when any other subsidiary is purchased, including entitlement to continuity of service and consequent redundancy provisions preserved. All other features are comparable to company purchases except that where assets have been transferred into the subsidiary within six years of its sale, there is a liability for capital gains tax and possibly also for development land tax. These liabilities fall on the purchased company for which roll-over relief is not available. Accordingly, a hive down is only likely to be considered where there is little capital gains tax liability, or where the assets on which it arises can be sold separately, so leaving the tax liability with the vendor.

Hiving down is particularly valuable where a company is otherwise unsaleable; some choice over its composition is essential, balancing charges need to be avoided and trade union opposition complicates a straight assets sale.

Demergers

To date, the demerger provisions of Section 117 of the Finance Act 1980 have been little used. During the first three years, the provisions are reported to have been used just fifteen times for all purposes, though this total includes some very large transactions. Only four of the financiers interviewed claim to have used demergers for any purpose, but encouragingly, several hoped to use them if an appropriate situation arose. Their advantages include the avoidance of virtually all tax and duty associated with the situation.

Demergers may be undertaken in three ways, but for practical purposes here they may be considered as the transfer of a subsidiary or a trade in return for shares from the purchaser which are directly distributed to the vendor's shareholders. Several conditions must be met in order to qualify, but most buy-outs should have little difficulty in meeting them. Perhaps the most important conditions are that the subsidiary must be at least 75 per cent owned by the vendor; investments or property must not be the main activities of the subsidiary; and that where a trade is distributed, little or nothing of it shall be left behind. The new company shall then have that trade as its sole or dominant activity and the purpose of the deal shall have been generally to benefit trade.

Once complete, the demerged company is restricted for five years on the distributions it makes. Essentially anything above a running yield issued for bona fide commercial reasons is disallowed. The Inland Revenue has wide powers of investigation on this point, backed with prohibitive penalties. Most buy-outs, however, will not be contemplating the distribution of capital through dividends. Thus the chief objection to demergers appears to be the initial requirement of settlement with equity.

Despite their theoretical attractions to many companies with complicated group tax problems which want to divest and return some capital to their shareholders, demergers are likely to be limited to very large buy-outs. Here the buy-out team may have only a small proportion of the equity, voting control may never be a possibility, and the merits of starting with a broad equity base are readily apparent.

The choice of a scheme

The most important factors by far in a choice of scheme are whether a deal can be done at all and the price which is finally agreed. Assets purchases may seem attractive at first but a company purchase, with all its problems, can be entirely justified by a favourable price whose negotiation has been simple and rapid. Asset purchases can produce problems if there are no historic taxable profits against which large capital allowances can be offset. The issue is similar to tax losses in companies. Cash flow will be critical in the opening months of trading, yet in many cases the actual benefits from the tax allowances will be nearly two years away.

8 After the buy-out

Suddenly the weeks, even months of negotiation are over; the doubts and the possibility of total failure at short notice have finally cleared. At last the events of the next few days no longer dominate the perspective with uncertainty and tension. Instead they are replaced with independence and the real prospect of accumulating substantial wealth. There may be a natural tendency to relax and generally reduce the pressure, but this should be resisted; the immediate phase is likely to be among the most important of the buy-out teams' entire business careers. Now is the time when the direction will be set and reputations with customers, suppliers and the workforce re-established. The neglect of the routine running incurred whilst the buy-out team were occupied elsewhere must be reversed.

Although the team's best efforts are called for, it should have become easier to meet the demands made of it. There is much to do but now the team has the authority to execute radical measures. The strained relationships and isolation experienced by many team members as a result of the numerous absences and secret meetings, are now likely to be far less telling following the assumption of control.

Non-executive directors

Furthermore, the team is not entirely on its own; the financiers will have insisted upon non-executive directors, probably in every case, and they are not there solely to protect the financiers' interests. One financier appoints a silver-haired chairman with experience of the industry and two non-executive directors as well, in recognition of the need for advice and to provide a general sounding board for the team in its transition to independence. If this is exceptional, then at least some exernal support can be expected which enables the team to become just that much more effective in the everyday running of the business.

The workforce

The extent to which the workforce has to be informed of the new development will depend largely on whether the buy-out scheme has been for assets and on the extent of unionisation. Whatever the previous state of knowledge, ensure that, on the first day, everyone is informed of who owns, and is now running, the business. In any briefing for employees, expect to provide full answers for the points of trivial, peripheral detail which arise from rumour and gossip.

Suppliers and credit rating

Also on the first day, it is essential to be prepared to

reassure customers and suppliers of the new organisation's financial standing and trading basis. Several approaches are possible although the best, a personal visit, may not be practical in many cases. Aside from contacting interested parties, the team must be prepared to receive contacts from some of them, and also from credit rating agencies. Decide in advance how much of the opening balance sheet is to be disclosed and who, among your bankers and accountants, is to be contacted for credit rating. With numerous opening balance sheets containing confusing information, it is essential to give an appropriate and correct impression.

Cash flow and budget development

A few buy-outs start with insignificant gearing or with lower gearing than the original organisation, but for everyone else the immediate prime concern will be with cash flow. The financing proposal will have contained cash flow forecasts and these are likely to have included the summarised cash flow for the first trading period and a detail schedule of month-by-month payments and receipts. Much time and work will have gone into these and unless they were prepared several months previously, they should represent the best set of forecasts and intentions the team can make at the start of independence. If a criticism can be made of them it is likely to be that, because the detail has been kept neat for the bankers, they may now be too brief for working documents. Suitable additions will consist of precisely those entries which can only be estimated broadly and so are likely to lead to variances. Large expense items, capital purchases and sales, tax payments and receipts, and the working capital entries are examples which justify a separate listing in order to exercise control and improve prediction. Elaboration of the original cash flow forecasts should be a simple matter.

As well as monitoring receipts and payments on a monthly basis, virtually all businesses will need a daily cash budget. This reflects receipts and the previous closing positions on the current accounts at the bank, while making an estimate of which payments are likely to be presented.

Even with adequate provision for working capital such a procedure should be started against the probability of a cash fluctuation later on. The other budgets which will be needed to run the business are unlikely to have been developed in sufficient detail. It may not have been possible to do so prior to the buy-out due to uncertainty over timing and the need for consultation outside the buy-out team. In preparing these budgets it is advisable to review the position audit and planning procedure. The former may benefit from the additional general information and from the initial market and supplier reaction to the buy-out. All aspects of the organisation should be covered: production and operations, personnel, systems and accounts. Particular attention should be given to marketing. This is the discipline which will most closely determine whether those sales forecasts and future corporate development plans will be met.

The planning horizon

Following the latest position audit it may be unnecessary to alter the business plan. However, in looking a matter of years ahead the plan many take insufficient account of immediate preoccupations which are expected to diminish in importance later. The effect of these is to bring the planning horizon forward for initial practical purposes from around three years to perhaps one and a half years at the most, with the prospect of returning to the longer view after the first year's trading. This can affect a variety of topics such as new investment, product development and market penetration, which are strictly necessary in the longer term but which can be given a lower priority in the meantime.

The budgets

There is no simple choice of the number and applications of the budgets. Too few will result in amateur management; too many will lead to aspects of bureaucracy with which most buy-out teams will be only too familiar. The budgets are influenced by the content of the business plan and the forecasts expressed or implied by it. They also depend on the organisational structure, who is involved and what is supposed to be happening. It is worth remembering that a budget can have several functions, some of which may not be immediately apparent. Perhaps six broad functions may be identified:

- Communication
- Setting objectives
- Activity co-ordination
- Responsibility allocation
- Motivation
- Performance appraisal

Budgets convey a great deal of information to their users in a business. Decide what they are saying and whether it should be restricted and, if so, to whom. Every budget is backed by a forecast. This may have been made and expressed formally or it may merely have the status of an ad hoc assumption. Whatever its form, the forecast will imply an objective which the budget sets. It is important to assess whether the period of the objective, whatever it might be, is consistent with the range of accuracy of the forecast. If a one year budget has a vast variance after two months it will fail to provide any realistic objective. Activity co-ordination is influenced by objectives and forecasts, but refers primarily to the correlation of subsidiary budgets. It is possible to have isolated budgets, but in general a budget which fails to co-ordinate will promote confusion. Responsibility allocation can be considerable from budgets, particularly where the organisational structure is neither clearly defined nor recognised. Ensure that those affected have the appropriate authority for their functions. Motivation is a complex issue affected by several issues which may include budgeting. By providing an opportunity for a measure of participation in the budgeting process it is possible to ease the budget's acceptance. Lastly, performance appraisal may result from the successful implementation of at least one of the five preceding functions.

Systems and statistics

The budgeting process will highlight numerous deficiencies which may or may not have been previously apparent. Systems, statistics, figures: all will be needed to produce budgets accurately and above all, rapidly. Many of these figures will not be available in situations where the management services of a larger group formerly operated. Question exactly what is needed before procedures are introduced. The organisation itself may need to develop in response to shortcomings indicated by budgets but at this stage changes should be confined to functions which are essential to the first year's business plan.

Developing the budgets

With an experimental budgeting process involving activities, objectives, forecasts and above all, people, numerous mistakes are inevitable in the limited time available. Some of these will disappear with time as forecasting and the collection of figures improves, but where there is no improvement or where a budget fails to achieve its intended purposes, the errors should be swiftly eliminated. Cases of hopelessly large variances can be expected in nearly all businesses in the first year but they should not be allowed to persist.

Buy-out team cohesion

Some financiers have expressed doubts over the cohesion of the buy-out team after the buy-out. A group has come together which may have little in common apart from being employed by the same organisation and having an interest in a deal. Following the deal there will be much enthusiasm and the pressure to establish the venture as a success, but later on the effects of recent substantial wealth, a changed management hierarchy and new responsibilities may bring the stability of the team into question. This is a minority opinion; others note that many teams with such a problem will have been dissuaded from ever starting or will have failed during negotiation. They consider the failure rate of team members as broadly comparable with conditions in other companies and notably less severe than with business start-ups. Nevertheless a high level of executive turnover is noted among those buy-outs which under-perform, a level which would have been higher had the UK experienced an economic downturn during recent years instead of a steady, if very slow, recovery from recession.

9 Four case studies of buy-outs

In order to show just what can be achieved through the buy-out process, four companies were selected and their chief executives interviewed, the chief executive being the buy-out team leader in each instance. Three of the companies are larger than average for buy-outs, whether rated by turnover, profits, number of employees or the initial consideration for their purchase; two of them are very much larger. The fourth company, however, is smaller than the average, so that, overall, their attributes illustrate buy-outs widely.

The studies have been written primarily to cover points relevant to buy-outs and much information for other purposes, such as investment appraisal, has been neglected. Nonetheless, if they are used for purposes other than buy-outs, it should be remembered that although written and completed with the full co-operation of the companies concerned, several opinions and forecasts remain the author's. Moreover, between mid-April and early May 1984 when the interviews were conducted for the three companies which have since gone public, the *Financial Times* Thirty Share index was around or above 900 and rising.

The author would like to thank Leo Liebster, Ian McCue, Jon Pither and Brian Taylor for the great help which they have given with the studies of their companies.

Amari PLC

Amari PLC is of great interest among buy-outs since, if current plans to obtain a public quote are realised, it may become the first public company to have been taken over, bought out by the management and taken to the market a second time. This cycle of control makes it an unusual case for examining some of the effects of differing ownership.

Originally founded in the early years of the century to mine tin in West Africa, Amari became incorporated in the 1930s and obtained a public quote. Its tin interests eventually started to run down and by the early 1960s it had become a shell company; in other words, its business had died away leaving the directors, certain assets and little more. Its modern history dates from 1962 when a metal distribution business was built up based on aluminium, but with interests in copper and stainless steel. At this time it also became a turnkey builder of metal forming plants[1]. The current Chairman and Managing Director, Jon Pither, joined the company in 1969, having worked for the group as a

---

[1]   A turnkey project is one constructed by a contractor completely so that the customer merely pays for it. The contractor later hands over the completed plant to the owner, who 'turns the key' and makes it work.

consultant since 1965. These were years of firm expansion for Amari.

Historically, the aluminium industry has been a difficult one in which to compete. Despite a long-term market growth rate which has been higher than for nearly all other metals, the vertically-integrated structure of the North American producers and their restriction of margins to discourage anti-monopoly measures traditionally combined to leave few competitive opportunities for others. The splitting up of the North American industry and the proliferation of production facilities elsewhere over the last forty years have steadily eroded the market power of the producers. Combined with the various pressures of the last fifteen years on multinationals to take profits at differing production stages, it is now much less easy, for example, to defend the producer price of ingot aluminium by squeezing margins on bauxite and semifabrications. These developments have helped to create the market opportunity for horizontally integrated companies such as Amari and may partly explain its rapid growth. Future developments in the industry will probably continue to favour horizontal integration of downstream activities.

After being the subject of sporadic takeover rumours for perhaps three years, Amari was eventually acquired in 1974 for £3.3 million by Selection Trust Ltd, a mining finance house. The sale was with the approval of the board, relations with the parent company were very good from the outset and over the next six years the question of senior executives leaving never arose. As a mining group with some direct interests in exploration and mining, as well as portfolio investments, the finance house lacked interests in wholesale and merchanting activities and these were met by Amari. After the takeover, the metal plant builder was taken out of Amari, but interests in aluminium extrusion, anodising, finishing, plastics stockholding and home improvements were added to the expanding stockholders. A considerable degree of independence was enjoyed by Amari and separate management functions maintained.

Ownership changed for the second time following the takeover of Selection Trust Ltd by an oil company in August 1980. This takeover was opposed by Amari's Board and the subsequent relationship with the parent company was never happy. The oil company appeared to be buying into mining and minerals simply to diversify, the business having little in common with its own strengths in oil exploration, production and shipping. After a year of the new ownership, the oil company's investments in minerals had hardly developed and Amari's Managing Director, Jon Pither, gradually realised that Amari needed a new home.

Trading results at this time were a disappointment. Turnover increased remarkably during the recession, but profits collapsed in the year ending 31 December 1980 and there was a loss the following year. Disregarding another loss-making subsidiary of Selection Trust, Hudsons Offshore Holdings Ltd, which was consolidated with Amari between 1980 and March 1982 for tax purposes, the decline can be related to lower margins in the recession on stockholding, to losses on aluminium extrusion in 1980 and 1981 and to losses on the diversification into home improvements between 1980 and 1983. Amari also suffered from the general reduction in trade credit and this, combined with the restricted capital programmes of 1980 and 1981 and with the current high interest rates, led to rising financial charges in the five years to 1982. The table opposite illustrates some of the figures through this difficult trading period. The figures have been adjusted to exclude Hudsons Offshore Holdings.

£,000	1978	1979	1980	1981	1982	1983
Turnover	55,731	71,392	83,986	92,566	111,205	136,609
Depreciation	592	874	1,158	1,323	1,558	1,145
Interest payable	640	852	1,070	1,308	1,772	1,568
Profit before tax	2,078	2,375	158	(1,741)	181	2,918
Retained profit	2,651	2,619	(119)	(2,058)	116	1,236

Though achieved against the circumstances of the oil company's ownership and the economic downturn, the losses specific to Amari appear to have played the greater part in the decline of 1980 and 1981. The subsequent slow recovery of margins may be attributed to changed circumstances, of which the oil company's ownership may have been a major feature.

The first step towards a buy-out was taken in the autumn of 1981 when Jon Pither approached two financiers to see if the broad outline of a scheme could be financed. One financier thought not, but the other, Midland Bank, the company's main banker, thought it might just be possible. With this encouragement, Jon Pither carefully started to sound out the reaction of the oil company to a divestment. The company showed considerable resistance to the idea in late 1981 and it took about six months of lobbying to establish that divestment was not only a suitable course, but that selling to the management might achieve an amicable exit. The first offer was made towards the end of 1982 and took the form of a staged buy-out, with proportions of the equity to be progressively acquired over several years. This was not accepted by the oil company and so it was followed by a simple cash offer early in 1983.

The syndicate of financing institutions had come together with Moracrest Investments as the lead financier. The initial lead financier had been Midland

Bank Industrial Finance, but the job was then assigned to Moracrest Finance Ltd, a subsidiary jointly owned by Midland Bank PLC, Prudential Assurance Co. Ltd, and British Gas Central Pension Schemes. Moracrest's investment management is handled by Midland Bank Industrial Finance. Moracrest's auditors were hired for much of the accountancy and another firm of accountants were engaged to deal with tax issues. Legal assistance came from some solicitors experienced in buy-outs while, to complete the professional advice, Amari's stockbroker provided valuable assistance over financing. The oil company finally accepted an offer of £5 million which was slightly higher than the initial cash offer and the buy-out was secured on 8 December 1983. The year which elapsed between bid and acceptance indicates the scale of difficulties involved. Numerous points which arose will be of wide interest.

In the spring of 1983, the oil company's reaction to the first cash offer had been entirely prudent. A merchant bank, a major member of the Accepting Houses Committee, was engaged to assess alternative divestment methods and a list drawn up of forty-five potential suitors for Amari. This proved to be quite a problem for Jon Pither. On the one hand there was difficulty sustaining the oil company's interest in the sale of a subsidiary whose total loss would scarcely scratch the balance sheet, while on the other hand, any takeover by a third party was fraught with uncertainty. Over a period of months, Jon Pither got the list reduced to thirty-five and then made it plain to undesirable candidates that they could not count on the senior management remaining with the company. A buy-out became the likely outcome from around the middle of the year.

From an early stage careful negotiations were necessary with several parties. A couple of banks supplying a minor part of the day to day banking arrangements decided to abandon a company which was proposing to leave an important oil company and they had to be replaced. Customers accepted the prospective change of ownership freely, but the suppliers needed some careful reassurance over the credibility of the buy-out. Some of the tax issues also needed time. A highly-praised scheme was drawn up by the tax accountants, but obtaining several valuation clearances from the Inland Revenue was time-consuming, apparently because the company was thriving. Amari Holdings PLC was incorporated in July and the following September was subscribed to by twelve founder shareholders, the seven board members and five other managers.

Amari had a huge advantage in having a management team which had worked together for several years. Some of the members had been independent in the past, management functions were complete and self-contained, and all had been united in their opposition to the parent corporation. Motivation towards the buy-out was thus positive and little or no personal adjustment was needed for independence. The workforce too appears to have perceived its interest as being in line with the management team. The shareholdings of the group of twelve were restricted in order to give wider participation and an invitation was issued to employees to subscribe towards the total of £1 million required for the purchase of 52 per cent of the equity. The issue was conducted through an offer and a subsequent rights issue, together bringing the minimum subscription to £864. Some employee share issues aimed at securing identity with the organisations have not had a minimum subscription. In this case it was decided to avoid the disadvantages of a huge share register and the dealing expenses of very small holdings. The issue was heavily oversubscribed and there was much competition for the allotment. Eventually the equity allocation was decided by Jon Pither and two colleagues and thereafter there was no trouble over its division.

The share capital raised for the buy-out was through cumulative redeemable convertible preference shares issued to the investing institutions, and through equity divided 52 per cent to the ordinary shares sold to the directors and employees, and 48 per cent to the preferred ordinary shares issued to the institutions, so giving the following interests:

	%
Moracrest Investments Ltd	16
ICFC Division of Investors in Industry plc	16
County Bank Ltd	8
West Midland County Council Superannuation Fund	8

The preferred shares had a fixed dividend of 10 per cent and the right to a further dividend of 12½ per cent of net profits in excess of £2.069 million once the preference shares were redeemed or converted. The preference shares carried an 11 per cent dividend and were redeemable in five tranches from net profits with priority over other distributions thus:

Redemption Date	Amount £'000
1 October 1985	500
1 October 1986	550
1 October 1987	600
1 October 1988	650
1 October 1989	779

In addition to the share capital, facilities for £23 million of working capital were arranged. Of this, £20 million are overdraft facilities and £3 million are a medium term loan. The latter is repayable over ten years starting in 1986.

The financial gearing introduced by this capital structure was high when set against the results for 1983, even if overdrafts are taken at the level of just over £9 million in the balance sheet. The implied cover for interest and grossed up dividends on the preference and preferred capital combined was less than two with operating profits at £4.486 million for the year ending 31 December 1983. However this type of analysis is slightly academic since the 1983 results are most unlikely to have shown the management in a favourable light with virtually the whole year spent negotiating a buy-out. Such a situation will be shared by most buy-out teams.

Also in common with most buy-outs, the opening balance sheet has points which the company will wish to strengthen. Once again, for the current year these should be seen in their appropriate context; a measure of neglect ahead of a buy-out valuation. Nevertheless, an improvement still has to be made and in particular to the funding of working capital.

It is debatable just how much working capital Amari needs. For any company in the wholesaleing business, working capital is likely to look exposed since a high figure for creditors is secured effectively on stocks. Apply a conventional ratio analysis to such a situation and at first sight there may be an unfavourable comparison with other commercial companies, but in fact it may reflect nothing more than good stock and cash control. Exactly how much working capital is really needed is partly influenced by the growth rate of sales with its implication for the growth of stocks. In Amari's case with some six weeks stocks held and working capital needs running at about one-eighth of the annual sales level, it is possible to see a sales growth rate of 10 per cent pa financed internally. The figure is reduced to 10 per cent pa since dividends, debt servicing and capital investment are making substantial calls on internally generated cash flow during 1984. Higher self-financed growth will be possible later when the gearing has been cleared out of the balance sheet and the efficiency of the organisation has been raised.

Current sales are very buoyant and are expected to rise in 1984 by more than the historic trend of 20 per cent compound to something in excess of £180 million. An improvement of margins, albeit to a level well short of the 3.6 per cent achieved in 1979, makes a gross profit of £5 million entirely feasible. Sales of this size suggest an additional working capital need of around £6 million, perhaps £5 million of it to be financed externally. Thus part of the success of the buy-out depends on Amari's financing strategy and ability to fund working capital of this order.

The issues raised by Amari's financing will be familiar to many buy-out teams. With significant further debt ruled out for a year or two by commercial prudence and with the potential for asset sales limited, the major alternative for funding will be to broaden the equity base. Another strategy might be to choose low growth and finance both working capital and twelve years of debt repayments out of cash flow, but the risks of such a policy are considerable: fewer resources would be built up and future recourse to the equity market would be jeopardised through the loss of any chance of attaining a premium rating. If there is ever any intention of obtaining a quote, the preferable course by far may be to grow, incur such a financing requirement as arises, but obtain a more favourable price for the equity by virtue of the growth.

An argument against expanding the equity is that voting control by the employees is almost certain to be lost. It will be lost if there is an offer for sale, and it is likely to be lost if there is a rights issue, unless all take up their rights. However, the eventual loss of control may be seen as inevitable if a quote is obtained, simply through a drift of transactions in a wider market towards outsiders. If this is to be the case, it may be preferable to arrange a flotation in a professional manner and at least secure some large institutional shareholders in the process.

Valuation is a problem with many recently purchased companies. For Amari, the question is not so much what it *is* worth as what it *would be* worth if the balance sheet was in order. If an issue, among other things, raised something in excess of £10 million from the market which was used to redeem the £3.08 million of preference shares, the balance going to working capital, the way would be clear for a substantial premium rating for the equity above the sectoral averages for stockholders, engineering and building products. After all when did you last see a compound growth rate of sales, during the recession, of 20 per cent pa and more from a company of Amari's size? There are few companies which can better this growth rate in any sector.

Amari obtained a full market quote in July 1984, shortly after this book had been completed. The issue was of 12.2 million shares, some 9.8 million of which were previously unissued, the balance being from existing shareholders. This represents 41.9 per cent of the total ordinary issued share capital. The institutional shareholders took the opportunity to lighten holdings by 15 per cent, the employees by 11 per cent and the directors by 8 per cent of their previous levels. At the issue price of 110p, the 9.8 million new shares raised roughly £10.1 million for the company after expenses. After the redemption of the preference shares, the remaining £7 million of capital will have solved the balance sheet problems at a stroke, since any remaining debt may be related to a much higher figure for current assets than appeared in the historic 1983 results.

In just seven months, Amari has all but removed the financial handicap introduced by the buy-out but more time will be needed before the exercise can finally be judged a success. For this, many observers are likely to want to see the next set of annual accounts and to be able to anticipate a further sales increase in 1985 allied to an improvement in margins, thereby demonstrating an enhanced management performance after a buy-out.

Sarasota Technology Ltd

Sarasota is unusual among buy-outs since most are not associated with new technology. The reasons are usually that new technology companies often have to sell at a premium to asset value and, in any case, they are readily saleable by methods other than a buy-out. The team is thus faced with competition for control, while facing difficulties in raising finance from institutions who hitherto have been reluctant to finance goodwill. Sarasota provides an excellent illustration of these points and may help to indicate future developments in this area.

The company was founded in the mid-1950s by an American, Merton Wilcox, at Sarasota, Florida. It was a small business start-up producing instrumentation for car parking and traffic control facilities. The market was large and by the mid-1960s, Merton Wilcox decided to expand with a UK production unit. Ian McCue, the 28 year-old chief engineer from a medium-sized company, was employed to start and run the new factory in 1966. Growth was organic and based on traffic products until the company diversified into measurement equipment for rivers and the water industry in 1978, and into control equipment for the process industry through the acquisition of J. Agar Instrumentation Co. in 1979. At present the company's business is based on these product lines, though further products may be expected in the future. By the time of the buy-out in April 1982, turnover was approximately £6 million and there were 230 employees spread across production units and organisations, in both the UK and US.

Ownership of the group started to become a matter for concern in the early 1970s due to the prospect of Merton Wilcox's retirement within a few years and the probable sale of the company. Ian McCue started to investigate the possibility of a buy-out in 1973 and approached several financing institutions, but it proved to be quite impossible to structure a deal under the conditions prevailing in 1973-74. Another attempt was made in 1976 to put a deal together as an alternative bid against the building materials group, Redland, who were interested in an acquisition. Once again, support for a buy-out was not available from the financiers who were approached and Redland gained control.

By this time Ian McCue had come to accept that a purchase by an external group was inevitable. The deal had a certain logic for Redland since they had invested in a US company involved in highway marking products and all Sarasota's output was going to the automatic parking and traffic control market. Additionally, Redland were interested in an introduction to electronics. With a self-supporting company like Sarasota who knows what the potential for synergy might be? With the value of hindsight, it proved to be distinctly limited, but at least no attempt was made to integrate the organisations. Sarasota was left as an intact group with its own management services. Redland proved to be an excellent employer as regards its personnel policies, but for Ian McCue the difficulties were the familiar ones of dealing from a small unit within a large corporation. When faced with an unfamiliar technology, decision-taking by the large group was uncharacteristically cumbersome.

At first it seemed that the problems were due to Sarasota's small size and this provided the incentive to acquire J. Agar Instrumentation. This company, too, had facilities in the UK and the US, was about the same size as Sarasota and was also run by a proprietor who wanted to retire. Redland provided the funds with exemplary speed and the acquisition was completed in three months. However it proved to make little difference for Ian McCue and by the middle of 1980, he had realised that what was really needed was a divestment. By chance it was possible to arrange to hold a routine Redland parent board meeting at Sarasota's offices, which adjoin the main works. With such an opportunity, Ian McCue used the occasion to show everyone at first hand how illogical it was to retain such a company in a building products group. The meeting was on 26 February 1981. Exactly one month later, the board decided to divest Sarasota and Ian McCue was notified directly.

In view of his previous unsuccessful attempts to finance a buy-out in the UK, Ian McCue immediately went to New York, where he spent a week putting his story to several US institutions, with mildly encouraging results. However a successful outcome was due to a UK banker who happened to be in the adjoining seat on the return flight. A meeting was arranged for the next working day in London and this led to a financing plan, to the engagement of solicitors, the employment of Sarasota's auditors as accountants and then to an initial offer to Redland in the mid-June 1981. In the meantime Redland had decided to examine alternatives to a buy-out. A New York firm of investment brokers had been commissioned to sell Sarasota and to take such steps as were necessary to decide on a divestment method, find potential purchasers and structure any deal. This programme soon required Ian McCue to put together a sale prospectus for any rival bidders. A number of serious enquiries were made, but all withdrew after considering the interests of the buy-out team in acquiring control.

Final completion of the buy-out was on 1 April 1982,

over ten months after the first offer. As Sarasota was a self-sufficient subsidiary which was being sold as a company, little or no difficulty was reported over technical details associated with the divestment, and no delay or difficulty was encountered with any Inland Revenue clearances. There was some apprehension among the workforce at one stage, but this was overcome through some careful consultation. The extended negotiations were mainly related to an inter-relationship between price, valuation and finance, with the credibility of the buy-out team as perhaps a secondary issue. The financiers needed reassurance on this latter point. Ian McCue had borne the buy-out arrangements virtually alone and, although the other Sarasota directors had been informed of the likelihood of a buy-out attempt just before the initial offer in June, with the implication that a team would have to be formed, it was not until December that negotiations were sufficiently far advanced for their outcome and the implications of control, independence and equity shares to be fully appreciated. The four months prior to completion were tense for the buy-out team and Ian McCue took the financiers on a tour of the company's facilities in the UK and US to build up the confidence of all parties concerned.

Price was perhaps the prime point of difference in negotiation. Redland's initial target was nearly three times the figure agreed nine months later, and Ian McCue's opening bid was roughly two-thirds of Redland's figure. Sarasota's break-up value rested on property worth just under £2 million with perhaps £½ million for working capital. On a going concern basis it might have been possible to justify a slightly higher figure but, whatever the detail, it was always clear that there would be substantial goodwill in the final price. The first financing house recognised this and had intended to handle the deal alone. However their proposal involved uncompetitive terms for the management team and, after some enquiries, they were replaced by Barclays Development Capital as the lead institution.

Although numerous financing institutions are believed to have looked at the deal, three syndicates involving five houses can be identified as interested, the most prominent being headed by Barclays Development Capital. There was another interested institution but this soon withdrew. Much later, one of the syndicates of two major houses also withdrew, creating an embarrassing gap at an advanced stage of the negotiations. The two remaining syndicates had a member in common, Equity Capital for Industry, which now played a valuable role in holding the various interests together. This led to one of the two remaining syndicate leaders, CIN Industrial Finance, part of the National Coal Board Staff Pension Fund, emerging as the leading institution in the negotiations and doubling their investment.

The final price was £5.4 million, a premium over book value of £1.376 million, yet far less than the figures initially discussed in negotiations. Considerable credit is due here to the financiers whose participation in negotiation greatly helped to achieve a reduced price. Although in other circumstances the company would be valued on the basis of a multiple applied to historic earnings, once goodwill was being considered different criteria came into play and it became necessary to form a view of how the goodwill had arisen and what it relied upon. Since the presence of an appropriately motivated management team forms possibly the most important single feature of goodwill, the value of this team may differ according to who buys the company. One price is appropriate to the management team who justify the goodwill; another price to other parties. With the imminent possibility of a sale to the buy-out team at a price just over one-third of Redland's opening offer, naturally there were some managers, due to be left behind, who were envious of the buy-out team. Against such a background, Ian McCue was anxious to complete as soon as possible.

The capital structure divided the equity into 'A' and 'B' shares, each of £1 nominal value fully paid-up. These were allotted as follows:

		Initial % of equity
Ian McCue	74,000 'A' shares	9.24
11 Sarasota employees	127,000 'A' shares	15.86
Barclays Industrial Development Ltd	150,000 'B' shares	18.72
Equity Capital for Industry	94,081 'B' shares	11.75
Equity Capital Trustee	55,919 'B' shares	6.98
CIN Industrial Investment	300,000 'B' shares	37.45
	801,000	100.00

There is a clause in the company's articles by which either 'A' or 'B' shares are converted into deferred shares without dividends if profits fail to reach or exceed respectively certain targets between April 1985 and the end of March 1987. As a result, the buy-out teams proportion could rise from 25.1 per cent to a maximum 40 per cent of the total current equity. The debt was structured between 10 per cent preference shares worth £1.3 million allotted to the financiers in proportion to their 'B' share holdings and two variable rate loans; a secured bank loan of £1.75 million and a debenture of £1.2 million, making a total funding, including the equity of £5.051 million. In addition there was a temporary overdraft facility to meet the balance of the £5.4 million purchase price. There are conversion terms on the preference capital but these, and other details of the debt, became academic when Sarasota obtained a quote in July 1984, and gearing was reduced to zero by a combination of internally generated cash flow and issue proceeds. (Details of the quote are given on p. 126.)

Sarasota's trading performance has been outstanding. Sales growth has risen on a compound trend of just under 20 per cent during the four years from 1980, reaching £8.443 million in the year ending 31 March 1984. Profits have been less stable, almost halving in 1982, but this is explained partly by the state of the world economy, but more importantly, by a shortage of executive time and energy during the period April 1981 to March 1982 when the buy-out was the dominant concern. Margins have subsequently recovered to over 25 per cent at the operating level which with a slightly lower interest charge, will be fully reflected below the line in 1983/84.

Future prospects for the group must allow for an increase of between one-quarter and one-third in internally generated cash flow, which will follow the elimination of the debt. A higher investment rate is in prospect and growth opportunities based on market development, new markets and new products all provide substance for a prediction of continuing growth at a slightly higher rate than in the past. Without a parent company there is no longer anyone else to blame for shortcomings. Responsibility has to be accepted and results in a group which is altogether more creative. Naturally, these factors will be reflected in Sarasota's investment rating. Naturally too the financiers will be making very substantial gains on their involvement with the company.

It is all too easy in a successful situation to forget, on reflection, the doubts and risks which had to be overcome. In Sarasota's case, the reflection is valuable since three large buy-out financiers actually declined to participate just two and a half years ahead of the group obtaining a quote. If there was innate prejudice against financing goodwill it was certainly misplaced. What may have been more important for them, though, could have been the implications of goodwill on the purchase price and the consequent level of gearing.

It was known at the outset that sales of assets would be negligible after completion, so that the gearing issue merely involved the servicing and redemption of the preference capital and £2.95 million of funded debt. The results for 1982/83 indicate comparatively modest gearing. Operating profits at £1.926 million cover interest charges and the grossed up preference dividend combined by 3.14 times. However this was in a year when Sarasota's trading performance flourished. In addition, the resulting cash in the balance sheet would have significantly reduced interest charges and the variable rate debt would have benefited from a background of falling interest rates in the second half of the year.

Had the faith in Ian McCue and his team by the prospective financiers in the autumn of 1981 been misplaced, and the 1982/83 results been similar to those of 1981/82, with operating profits of around £1-£1.1 million, the gross cost of debt service would have been roughly £0.72 million with interest rates on the debt at 16 per cent. Had rates averaged 19 per cent, possibly the more plausible assumption under the conditions of autumn 1981 when financing was considered, the cost of debt service would have been £0.81 million; a level at which Sarasota might have been viewed as a marginal enterprise and certainly in no condition either to repay its debt from cash flow, or to make a successful flotation. Alternatively, had a middle view been taken by the financiers with interest rates of 17 per cent and with operating profits in

1982/83 showing a modest improvement to, say, £1.4 million, the cover on the debt service would have been twice.

This exercise may help demonstrate why, even with confidence in the buy-out team, albeit tempered by a measure of banker's conservatism, it would have have been difficult to justify a purchase price significantly in excess of £5.4 million and why there were problems in financing even this figure. Compared with other buy-outs, the price was high when set against book value. It was very high in relation to group turnover. Yet in just over two years the debt has been eliminated, much money has been made for the equity holders and the business itself is thriving.

As chance would have it, Sarasota obtained a full quote in the same week during July 1984 as Amari PLC. The issue was preceded by a capital reconstruction through which 226,714 'B' shares were re-designated as deferred shares; the remaining 'B' shares, together with all of the 'A' shares, were split into 10p shares. Further capital was also authorised. Of the 5.9 million shares issued at 132p, 2.7 million came from the buy-out team and the financing institutions and represented a reduction of 19 per cent in their holdings. The company itself raised approximately £3.4 million after expenses and had cash balances of £1.2 million after redemption of the preference shares and repayment of the debenture.

The issue may be seen as preparing Sarasota for fresh developments and growth. A small acquisition was made for shares concurrently with the issue and, although there was a statement accompanying the prospectus that further acquisitions were unlikely before the end of 1984, they are evidently a distinct prospect thereafter. Thus the company is moving on to fresh objectives unhindered by historic detail in the balance sheet.

Stratford Colour Company Ltd

Stratford Colour Company was formed from the buy-out of a factory at Stratford, East London, which was formerly part of the Burrell Colours Group. Burrell Colours was a small producer of a variety of types of pigments and colours which adopted a growth strategy in the 1970s more appropriate to the markets and trading conditions of the previous decade. Corporate procedures better suited to a larger organisation were adopted and by 1979 overheads were running at around £2 million, some 20 per cent or so of turnover of £9.9 million. Had sales developed as expected, this level of overheads might have been carried, but as it was, the cumulative effects of low profitability and the implications of inflation for working capital had affected liquidity. Net current liabilities of £0.9 million in the balance sheet at 31 December 1979 included an overdraft of £2.9 million. Several attempts were made to sell the company and negotiations reached an advanced stage, but conditions worsened rapidly following the economic downturn in 1980 and Burrell Colours was placed in the hands of a receiver in August of that year.

The following month, the finance director of Burrells, Leo Liebster, started to investigate the idea of a buy-out for one of the three factories. Leo Liebster had joined the company in 1977 having previously been finance director of another group. The idea of purchasing the Stratford factory had first arisen soon after he joined. The factory was loss-making; it produced lead chrome pigments for which the market appeared to be static and a report from the Alkali Inspectorate on pollution indicated the need to invest £250 000. At the trading level, however, the factory was profitable. The provisional case to sell it was based on figures which included overheads so that its survival, like the group as a whole, was associated with the essentially separate task of overhead reduction. A possible sale was thus deferred.

Now that a buy-out was being considered, the problem of overheads could be solved at a stroke. However, the viability of the venture could be jeopardised by the need for investment to meet pollution controls. A much closer look at the measures which were likely to be needed revealed that the earlier estimate of a 'quarter of a million' was much too high. In the event, some new ducting and a new stack has raised standards to the necessary levels at a cost of £23 000, an interesting contrast between entrepreneurial and corporate solutions.

The four-man buy-out team, including Leo Liebster and a solicitor, met in October 1980 and four financiers were approached. Discussions took place at an initial cursory level with one financier, there was one refusal and two offers, one of which was uncompetitive. CIN Industrial Investments Ltd, working through Development Capital Group Ltd, emerged as the lead financier and provided all professional help except for legal advice. The first offer to the Receiver was made in October and completion came in January 1981.

One advantage for the team lay in an indication from the Receiver that a purchaser would be favoured who ensured at least some continuity of employment at Stratford. However, the extent to which the team might continue to be favoured if a competitive bid developed was never clear and, in the end, the price was probably unaffected by social issues. Certainly, the team was apprehensive about the possibility of a counter-bid. It was considered at the time that such a move could only have come from a competitor wanting to eliminate capacity. In this connection, the break-up value would be relevant and it is interesting that even in the case of a small buy-out it was difficult to assess this figure accurately.

While the final price of £257 950 represented a discount on the asset value including stocks, it was probably a premium on any likely realisation for the site alone at the end of 1980, even including the very small amounts the plant would have realised in a forced sale.

The scheme used for the buy-out was a hive down and no outstanding problems of valuation or tax arose. Although the scheme need not have involved making all of the workforce redundant, the team insisted that this should be done and the costs fall on the Receiver. In August 1980, forty-five persons had been employed at the factory, perhaps thirty-five of them directly on production; by January 1981 the total payroll, including the three executive members of the buy-out team was only thirty, so that the production workforce was substantially reduced.

Perhaps the outstanding difficulty the buy-out team encountered was in overcoming the relative neglect of the business during the period of nearly five months when it was controlled by the Receiver. There had been no promotion of lead chrome pigments and, of those established customers who did come back to their traditional supplier, there was service only for those with a very good credit rating. This resulted in much damage to the customer base which took time to rebuild. Although this was a problem, it must be seen in the context of the price realised for the business. If the business had been trading more actively, it might have been possible to ask more for it.

A total of £505 000 was raised by the buy-out team. £253 000 was a secured debenture from CIN Industrial Investments Ltd at 14 per cent; £195 000 was raised from 10 per cent cumulative convertible redeemable participating preference shares; the remaining £57 000 as ordinary shares split thus:

	£
L.M. Liebster	25,649
One team member	9,119
Two others with one share each	2
CIN Industrial Investments Ltd	22,230
	57,000

In addition to their 10 per cent dividend, the preference shares qualify for a proportion of profits if these are in excess of £50 000 gross, the exact proportion being on a sliding scale until £450 000 pa is reached. With redemption by 1 January 1988, conversion of the preference capital to ordinary shares is triggered if the aggregate cumulative level of gross profit falls below threshold levels for each of the years up to 31 December 1985. Conversion terms are such as to give CIN Industrial Investments 51 per cent of the voting equity if this performance is not achieved.

The success of the buy-out has hinged on marketing. World capacity greatly exceeded sales in 1981 and still does. The major markets for lead chrome pigments are heavily dependent on the level of industrial expenditure but, although this has recovered slightly, any increase has been offset by the loss of certain markets such as printing ink. The buy-out team expected a static market and planned accordingly. A new range of lead chrome pigments was introduced and an emphasis placed on export sales. At the beginning sales were made to 18 overseas countries; but now the total is forty-eight, with perhaps 70 per cent of turnover from these sources. This volume increase has been at the expense of competitors' sales and had prices held to their 1981 levels, the buy-out would be highly profitable by now. Unfortunately the price of pigment has slipped from £1 700 per ton in 1981 to £1 300 per ton in 1984. Gross margins slipped from 12.8

per cent in 1981 to 5.8 per cent the following year and are unlikely to have recovered significantly in 1983. Internally generated cash flow, after meeting the preference divided, is just over £50 000.

The capital requirements of the business depend largely on measures taken to diversify away from lead chrome pigments. Significant moves of this nature, together with repayments of the loan and preference shares, take the minimum need for funds to around £100 000 pa over the next few years. While the generation of a figure of this order is fully within the capability of the company, provided that there is at least some recovery in the price of the product, current trading conditions leave the company viable but raise the question that some of this finance must be obtained externally.

From a national standpoint, Stratford Colour Company is a successful buy-out. A productive facility has been preserved, much of its employment has been maintained and, despite a deterioration in its market, it is currently a viable organisation. And this has been achieved without the official encouragement or support which is available in the nearby Docklands Development Area. A comparison of the implied return on the equity investment with the rates achieved at Amari and Sarasota, however, would be unfavourable to Stratford Colour, yet this feature may be closer to the experience of many buy-outs. Many situations are not expected to make a great deal of money. There is risk, there is financial gearing and in the event, the market moves against the buy-out. The team is then faced with a long period during which the company's relative competitive strength must be improved against a background of financial stringency. Many may identify with such conditions.

Wardle Storeys Ltd

Wardle Storeys was formed in February 1983 from the

amalgamation of two long-established plastics manu-
facturers. One of the companies, Bernard Wardle & Co
Ltd., had been established in 1908, became a publicly-
quoted company in 1946 and was eventually acquired
in March 1980 through the private interests of a well-
known entrepreneur, who will hereafter be referred to
as 'the entrepreneur'. These private interests were
later sold to another group in April 1982 and a buy-out
was then mounted under the leadership of the
Managing Director of Wardles, Mr Brian Taylor.
Following completion in October 1982, Brian Taylor
proceeded to purchase the second company in the
group, Storeys Industrial Products Ltd. This company
can trace its history back to the nineteenth century
with involvement in plastics manufacture from 1885. In
1977 it had been purchased by a major UK industrial
corporation and it was from this group that the
acquisition by Wardles was completed in February
1983. Between October 1982 and January 1984, the
group was known by the name of the buy-out holding
company, Wardby Ltd., the current name being
assumed at the latter date.

The group manufactures a wide variety of plastic
products of which the most important are plastic
sheeting and coated fabrics such as vinyl leathercloth.
Processes and procedures do not merit the term 'high
technology' or anything approaching it, but there is
much scope for product differentiation through design
and the orientation of output to changing market
needs. Active marketing policies are essential and all
of these efforts are directed towards industrial markets
and customers. Sales are spread across many sectors
with the automotive industry being by far the most
important. Four years ago the automotive industry
took over half of Wardle's sales, but this proportion
declined from 1980 and then fell much further to
around 30 per cent of sales after the acquisition of
Storeys.

The events which led to the buy-out may be

considered as starting in the late 1970s when Brian Taylor, who at that time was a manager with a company in another sector, decided he just had to try to become independent. He put a deal together on a different company and approached the entrepreneur referred to above. The response was favourable and the deal put in train, but, as is the nature of such things, it just happened to fall through. Soon afterwards, however, the entrepreneur came back to Brian Taylor to ask him to sort out a little local difficulty in a company he had just acquired. Brian Taylor joined Bernard Wardle as Managing Director early in May 1980. At the time he was 47.

The little local difficulty proved to be substantial. True, the recession was taking place at the time, but this appears to have been the least of the company's problems. Irrespective of the recession, Bernard Wardle had been heading for trouble since mid-1979. The company was already heavily dependent on the automotive sector and there was severe overcapacity in plastic products in Western Europe, when a change in fashion occurred in vehicle upholstery away from leathercloth and towards fabric finishes. Several adverse aspects of marketing were thus compounded at the same time. A further complication had been introduced at Wardles by diversification policies which included some engineering and garden products. The timing of these was ill-judged, but this is a view taken with the advantage of hindsight. More important was the lack of any marketing knowledge or tradition in the new product areas.

Brian Taylor spent his first fifteen months rationalising and stemming losses until, by the middle of 1981, the position could be considered as stabilised. Although the company was profitable at the operating level, it was still making a small net loss. The damage done to the balance sheet by the period of heavy losses had resulted in increased borrowing which, combined with the high interest rates of the day, had left a severe financial charge. Total borrowings had increased from just under £4 million in 1979 to a peak of just under £6 million in 1981 and, although they had fallen slightly, still remained high at £5 million. Moreover, within this latter figure, a term loan had been changed to overdraft. Creditors were pressing, the banks were anxious, the parent company was reluctant to advance further cash and, in all, over £5 million had been lost in 18 months when turnover was running at an annual rate of £24 million.

Realising that a full turnround would require rationalisation not just of Bernard Wardle but of most of the UK plastic products industry too, the acquisition of the major competitor, Storeys Industrial Products, was first mooted in the summer of 1981. All interested parties appear to have viewed the idea favourably, but Wardles were short of cash, the entrepreneur did not want a greater commitment to manufacturing and so a purchase was out of the question. Indeed a doubt was placed over Wardle's future financing for any purpose. Against this background, Brian Taylor had to look for an alternative and eventually started to screen the possibility of a management buy-out.

At first the weakness of the balance sheet appeared to rule out such a course. Net assets had come down from 11.2 million at the end of 1979 to 3.6 million by March 1981 and by the autumn the recovery had yet to start. Inevitably, there were doubts over whether a viable business could be supported. In addition, there were no assets available to be sold to help with the financing. About twelve financiers were approached and all but two turned the proposition down. There was little to choose between the two provisional offers and the choice was all the more difficult because it had to be made on broad issues which were dependent on details which would only be known once negotiations reached an advanced stage. Would the unsuccessful financier have been better? Brian Taylor will never know, but in any event the lead financier chosen,

Citicorp Development Capital, proved to be very satisfactory.

A first buy-out offer was made to the entrepreneur shortly before Christmas 1981. It was met with great interest but was turned down for that time-honoured reason among abandoned buy-outs, namely that a massive book-loss would be quite unacceptable in the parent company's accounts. This problem seemed insuperable and appeared to rule out the divestment of Wardles for the foreseeable future, if not indefinitely. Soon, however, the position was totally altered by another group acquiring the entrepreneur's holding company. Here was a new owner who actually wanted to realise some assets. Immediately a buy-out could be mounted to a willing vendor. The lead financier assembled three other investors: Electra Investment Trust, British Rail Pension Fund and Fountain Development Capital, which is run by the merchant bank Hill Samuel. It also engaged a major firm of accountants to investigate Wardles and its industry sector, a study which was made available to all four investors, to Wardles' clearing bank and to the buy-out team. Having operated alone hitherto, Brian Taylor had now brought in two team members, engaged another firm of accountants for tax advice and a leading firm of solicitors for the corporate legal work. Within the month of April, 1982, the first offer was lodged.

Completion came the following October. Over the intervening months, several changes were made to the terms of the offer and to the price, which finally differed substantially from its opening position. Negotiation was complicated and at times fraught, with any of the several interests being defended by the appropriate party. The lead financier took an active part and there is much praise for their performance, having as it did a material effect on the final deal and on the price obtained.

Two complications in raising finance had been,

firstly, that the business plan included the purchase of Storeys Industrial Products and, secondly, the group appeared to the financiers to have dubious commercial prospects. Having obtained a strong commitment on the finance, however, these two factors became very much to the buy-out team's advantage, as they facilitated the rapid reorganisation of most of the sector and helped to make it appreciated that the alternatives were either for the companies to be run by Brian Taylor and the team, or else by no-one, a far less favourable prospect for customers, suppliers, bankers and the workforce. No rival bid appeared, nor did one ever seem likely. No UK group seemed remotely interested in handling the situation and the best prospect for a rival bid, one of the European producers, was never considered, possibly since such a move could only have been justified to close capacity. An underlying factor may have been that, as already discussed, there were few surplus assets available for sale to offset some of the financing. The buy-out team itself had forecast little effect from this source and so it proved to be later on.

Relations with customers and suppliers at Wardles created no difficulties at all. After the darker days a year earlier with the company paying slowly, the new developments were identified as progress. At Storeys on the other hand, creditors needed much reassurance over the prospect of the company leaving a well-known group. The speed of the Storeys deal may have played a part here. Serious talking started on completion of the Wardles buy-out in October 1982, a statement of intention was made in December and completion followed in February 1983. Surprisingly, no problems were reported from the workforce, despite the heavy redundancies in prospect.

The total price for the two companies appears to have been just under £4.7 million. Of this, some £2.8 million were agreed redundancy payments for part of the Storeys workforce, leaving £1.2 million for the actual purchase of Storeys and £0.7 million for Wardles. The purchases were financed by a secured loan of £2 million, preference shares and equity totalling £2.02 million, proceeds from the sale of fixed assets coming to just £237,000 and the remainder from cash flow and short-term borrowing.

The initial capital structure was complicated by an elaborate incentive for the buy-out team whereby some of the capital could be converted to voting equity if a profit target were not met in the two years to 31 August 1984. This did in fact happen. If, on the other hand, a total of £3.694 million had been made before interest and tax over this period and all the other preference capital had been redeemed first, then the convertible redeemable equity could have been redeemed too. After full redemptions of redeemable capital, the remaining capital structure was:

1 *The management's equity:* 51 per cent of the total obtained for £83,500 and split: 83.8 per cent Brian Taylor, 5.4 per cent each to two members, 5.4 per cent divided among seven others.
2 *The financing investors' equity:* 49 per cent of the total obtained for £80,224 and split equally among:
    Citicorp Capital Investors Ltd
    Electra Investment Trust PLC
    Railway Pension Investments Ltd
    Fountain Development Capital Fund

By the time of the buy-out in October 1982, the rationalisation of Wardles was largely complete. Its turnover had been reduced to an annual rate of £19 million from £24 million two years earlier and this had been achieved through the closure of two factories, the disposal of a Dutch subsidiary and of the diversifications into engineering and garden products. Costs and general efficiency had been improved by measures which could have gone ahead irrespective of the scale of activities. These included the closure of the group head office and widespread workforce reductions. But most important of all had been the improved handling of working capital and in particular of stock turnover.

Storeys was much the larger organisation when it was purchased, with an annual turnover of perhaps £28 million. However, part of the purchase agreement was that one of the two main plants would be disposed of and this was contributing £14 million of the total. To say that this was the actual capacity reduction could be misleading since some equipment and processes were transferred to other factories in the group. Furthermore, there were considerable redundancies at the other Storeys plant and adjustments elsewhere; but the figures do at least indicate the scale of the reorganisation. The combined workforces of Wardles and Storeys totalled around 1900 at the start of 1983. A year later the figure was 1270, most of the redundancies at this time falling on Storeys.

There was much scope for cost reduction in combining administrations and salesforces and, by the end of 1983, the integration of the two businesses was largely complete. Rationalisation of product lines had started ahead of the Storeys acquisition, but subsequently the opportunities here, which had been a prime reason for the purchase, were greatly increased and continue at the present time with expansion of a number of higher-margin items. On-going cost reduction will include improved raw material usage.

The speed with which the reorganisation was undertaken is partly reflected through the balance sheet at the year end 31 August 1983. Net current assets stood at £4.72 million against net current liabilities at year end 1982 of £2.718 million, a change involving, inter alia, the elimination of the overdraft and short-term loans and the accumulation of £140,000 cash. The improved control of working capital had been the major influence, with internally-generated cash flow making a secondary, if rising, contribution. Only £237,000, as already mentioned, had come, in all, from fixed asset sales and interestingly, the tax losses incurred two years earlier by Wardles had no effect on the cash flow of this period. Amounting to over £5 million gross, these will have a valuable impact on cash flow in 1984, 1985 and 1986, but in the opening months of independence, they provided no benefit at all.

Just as the economic downturn in 1980 had been a minor factor in Wardle's fortunes, so the recovery which continued through the summer of 1984 was of no great consequence for Wardle Storeys. An expected sales level of £40 million in the year to 31 August 1984 reflects a slight demand increase, but for all practical purposes, Brian Taylor and his team had to reorganise the group against a static market. Further ahead, there is scope for expansion into new markets but perhaps the best guide to future strategy is the group's proven skill at turning round mature, medium-sized businesses.

A public quote was planned for late in 1984 and occurred that November. The initial market value placed on the company was expected to reflect the current rate of trading profits in excess of £2 million per year, the fact that 1984/85 was the first full year's trading after the reorganisation, the several aspects of ongoing potential in current activities and the continued strengthening of the balance sheet. With the cash position rising, the financiers were approached at the start of 1984 for the early redemption of £800,000 of preference stock, to which they agreed. The balance to be redeemed, just under £1 million, could easily be covered by current cash flow, as too could much of the £2 million loan. The situation makes an interesting comparison with the position in 1982 when the options for the companies appeared to be a sale to Brian Taylor and his team or nothing.

10 Conclusions

At this stage it is possible to draw a few conclusions from the book as a whole. These are not comprehensive but rather they are points which have arisen, typically in discussion, which are sufficiently important to justify coverage twice over.

Much has been made in this book of the wealth which can be created through buy-outs yet, in looking more closely at their complexity and at the time and trouble which busy executives have to spend over several months in order to achieve a buy-out, they emerge in the end as deserving caution and careful consideration, even in situations which ultimately are successful. There are also some out-and-out failures which few want to think about and no one wants to identify with. Thus while the rewards may be there, they have to be seen in a context of risk, time, work, pressure and expense. Necessarily, therefore, a business may need to look cheap to justify a buy-out, with a price substantially below the level at which a rational assessment would judge a venture as inadvisable on commercial grounds. Money is made at buy-outs, but it has to be made in order to justify the exercise.

In theory, many buy-outs can be taken to the first offer stage very rapidly, but in practice they are more likely to be mounted over a period of months. Professional advice will be essential and, in most cases, the earlier it is taken, the better it will be. Advice may be needed on accountancy, legal matters and on much company secretarial information which has received little coverage in this book. Above all, help on tax must be anticipated. To take a rule of thumb: if aspects of tax come to dominate a business proposal then the course may be inadvisable and should be closely reconsidered. Buy-outs are an exception to this rule. Tax issues may be expected to influence the viability of the buy-out, to determine the buy-out scheme, to provide the major points of difference in the negotiations and to introduce a component of residual risk through tax indemnities. The latter in particular can be controversial and cut across a conventional banker's view of liability and financial motivation for the buy-out team. Professional advice will be essential.

Several conditions are necessary to justify taking the idea for a buy-out through to an offer. One condition which is common to all buy-outs, and which will persist until the completion, concerns the possible departure of the proposed buy-out. The nature of the problem changes as the buy-out progresses. Initially it may be influenced by questions of strategy and the interaction of the business with the rest of the group, and also whether the climate of opinion among the parent company's board might be open to the idea of an offer. Many decisions both for and against such sales will be taken for unspoken reasons and at an early stage it may be impossible to assess an outcome.

Later the price will affect the issue and here it is not so much a matter of how an offer compares with a formal valuation as how it differs from what the parent company thought the value might have been which determines the opposition to a sale. Later still there is the possibility of obstruction from those in the parent company who gain nothing from the deal, who may lose some authority and who, in any event, will be left behind. All of these factors can block the departure of the buy-out.

For some bankers the really important aspects of the buy-out are not centred on the mechanics of the business or the scheme but rather on the people forming the team. Some of the issues involved in finding a good team and backing it raise questions about entrepreneurship which have been given considerable coverage in this book. Some interviewees have placed even greater stress than this book gives on the importance of entrepreneurial qualities in at least one team member. There is room for debate over just what constitute entrepreneurial qualities and an attempt has been made in Appendix 3 to clarify some of the literature. Mention must be made here of the persistence and drive needed even by those who prove to be successful. This may be partly assessed from the time spans between the first idea for the buy-out and the first offer, with other problems along the way contributing to the picture. After seeing much money made quickly in some buy-outs, it is all too easy to conclude that anyone could have done it and so overlook some of the personal qualities which were essential to the team's achievement.

Finally, it is valuable to consider when a buy-out becomes a success. At completion, most have a sense of unfinished business about them; there is exposure to risk, personal finances are stretched and there is much to be done. The criteria for success are debatable. Since success is open-ended it is an even more difficult term to handle than failure and, as the introduction noted, a successful buy-out from several standpoints need have only limited aims, such as providing economic activity and employment for perhaps as little as five years. Some more demanding criteria are now suggested since most of those buy-outs which succeed will obtain a public quote and then compare themselves, and be compared with, all other companies of a similar size and range of activities. To do this, most will need at least a full year's trading, and possibly several, with a performance which leads to a balance sheet in which the financial gearing is no longer the dominant concern. Such scope as there is for asset sales, issues of equity and so on will have been used imaginatively. In such a business, the debt advanced by financiers for the buy-out will have made its projected return, much if not all of it will have been repaid, the buy-out team will have been able to consider diversifying their portfolios and it will now be possible to set some fresh objectives for the organisation which are unrelated to the buy-out.

Appendix 1
Acknowledgements

To clarify numerous issues, interviews were carried out with some financiers who are active in buy-outs. Twenty-three houses were approached; nineteen were interviewed, two of them over the telephone, seventeen in person. The following gave most generously of their time and information.

M.R. Cumming,
Barclays Development
    Capital Ltd,
Chatsworth House,
66/70 St Mary Axe,
London EC3A 8BD.

D. Wills,
Charterhouse Development
    Ltd,
65 Holborn Viaduct,
London EC1A 2DR.

C.R.E. Brooke,
Candover Investments Ltd,
4/7 Red Lion Court,
London EC4A 3EB.

D. Prosser,
CIN Industrial Finance,
33 Cavendish Square,
London W1M 0AL.

J. Moulton,
Citicorp Development
    Capital,
33 Melbourne Place,
London WC2R 1HB.

C. Bloomfield and
    A. Davison,
County Bank Ltd,
11 Old Broad Street,
London EC2N 1BB.

N. Falkner,
Development Capital Group
    Ltd,
88 Baker Street,
London W1M 1DL.

M.C. Stoddart,
Electra Risk Capital,
Electra House,
Temple Place,
Victoria Embankment,
London WC2 R3 HP.

J.A. Lorenz,
Equity Capital for Industry,
Leith House,
47/57 Gresham Street,
London EC2V 7EH.

A. Hawksley,
Granville & Co,
27/28 Lovat Lane,
London EC3R 8EB.

T.A. Jones,
Gresham Trust Ltd,
Barrington House,
Gresham Street,
London EC2V 7EH.

J. Davis,
Guidehouse Ltd,
Vestry House,
Greyfriars Passage,
Newgate Street,
London EC1A 7BA.

Miss S. Palmer,
D. Sach,
ICFC Division,
Investors in Industry PLC,
91 Waterloo Road,
London SE1 8XP.

J.R. Beevor,
Midland Bank Industrial
    Finance Ltd,
22 Watling Street,
London EC4M 9BR.

G.T.A.W. Horton,
Minster Trust,
Minster House,
12 Arthur Street,
London EC4R 9BH.

M. Davidson,
Samuel Montagu & Co Ltd,
114 Old Broad Street,
London EC2P 2HY.

D.G. Hutchings,
Moracrest Investments Ltd,
22 Watling Street,
London EC4M 9BR.

R.J.C. Hamilton and
    S. Rhodes,
Pegasus Holdings Ltd,
11/15 Monument Street,
London EC3R 8JV.

R.P. Corbett,
Singer and Friedlander Ltd,
21 New Street,
Bishopsgate,
London EC2M 4HR.

In addition, three firms of accountants known to be active in buy-outs were approached. All were interviewed and were most helpful.

L.R. Blackstone,
Blackstone, Franks, Smith &
    Co,
388/396 Oxford Street,
London W1N 9HE.

A.F. Mills,
Spicer & Pegler,
Newater House,
Newhall Street,
Birmingham B3 3NY.

J.R. Hustler,
Peat, Marwick, Mitchell &
    Co,
1 Puddle Dock,
London EC4V 3PD.

Appendix 2
The Management Buy-Out Association

Management buy-outs now have their own association which holds regular meetings, compiles and circulates a register of buy-out practitioners and other professional advisers, and generally publishes information on buy-outs of interest to members. It can also act as a pressure group to lobby for improvements in legislation. Membership, which currently stands at over 110, is drawn from financiers, professional advisers and members of buy-out teams. The annual subscription is £25 and enquiries should be made to:

The Management Buy-Out Association Ltd,
388-396 Oxford Street,
London W1N 9HE.

Appendix 3
The entrepreneur in economics and entrepreneurial psychology

The neglect of the entrepreneur in economic theory

Traditionally, those who have wanted to study topics such as the creation of wealth, national economic growth and resource allocation have turned to the subject of economics. This would cast some light on the matter in hand and if its implications fell short of a complete appraisal or solution, then at least the areas of doubt, ignorance and speculation would be narrowed, often substantially so. On some topics there has been a notably less satisfactory treatment for a number of reasons; practical measures might be heavily influenced by actual conditions, there could be conflict and confusion between theories, or simply a shortage of theory. That is not to say that economics has nothing to contribute on such a topic, but merely that it has less of consequence. Inflation could be taken as an example and so can entrepreneurship.

Currently, most economists are likely to agree with one of the opening statements of M. Casson (1982)[1] that at the present, there is no established theory of the entrepreneur. Casson proceeds to deliver in his book rather more than his statement might be taken to imply, but nevertheless there is a shortfall of theory on entrepreneurs, although the position is notably better than it was even fifteen years ago. One reason for the lack of an established theory is, as was indicated by H. Leibenstein (1968), that economic theory assumes that the complete set of inputs to the production function are specified and known to all actual or potential firms. This assumption arises essentially from the emphasis classical economics places on equilibrium positions towards which the various facets of the economy adjust. At equilibrium, there is perfect dissemination of information. A second reason for the theoretical neglect of entrepreneurship, also indicated by Leibenstein, is the rarely challenged assumption of a fixed relationship between the inputs and outputs of firms. This too can be related to analytical theory which is organised around equilibria.

The effects of these assumptions have been to raise doubts over the nature and activities involved in entrepreneurship. Thus one general result of assuming free access to all information is, as Casson (1982) has pointed out, that decision-taking is trivialised in economic theory. Another result is that the entrepreneurial role itself is seen as being of passing relevance, since at equilibrium, it has no further functions to perform. Furthermore, where it is accorded a role of

---

[1] Two books appeared in 1982, within a few months of each other, on the entrepreneur in economic theory. Both have the same title and both are to a standard which should ensure their places as definitive works for many years. Their approach differs. R.F. Hébert and A.N. Link (1982) has the structure of a historical review while M. Casson (1982) is addressed primarily to problems and issues.

consequence and value, it is possible to attribute to it some misleading qualities. Take, for example, the implication that the entrepreneurs' discretionary powers are used to maximise profits. There need not necessarily be an implication that entrepreneurs are motivated solely by money, but such a deduction is usually taken nonetheless and typically, it will provide an erroneous view of the entrepreneur, his motives and activities.

Difficulties over identifying entrepreneurship

These reasons alone are sufficient to explain the entrepreneur's relative neglect in economic theory and some of the recurring confusion over definitions of entrepreneurial and managerial functions. That such a state of affairs could have arisen may be attributed in turn to the lack of a statistical definition of entrepreneurship. Had there been some positive quantity which theory had to accommodate, it might have been difficult to overlook. Remarkable though this proposition may seem, it should be remembered that a comparable attitude runs through most of commerce and accountancy. If you cannot put a number on something, it does not matter. If you can, it matters down to the last wretched penny.

The impossibility of assessing entrepreneurship as an independent variable has been referred to by R.M. Solow (1957). In considering a time series for economic growth, so much growth could be related to an increase in capital, so much to technical change, so much to entrepreneurs and the remainder to any other factors. Distinguishing the several operative influences from each other might just be possible if entrepreneurship was a discrete variable, but it is not. It qualifies most, if not all, of the other operating factors. Capital for instance may rise, but its use and actual quantity depend on a certain entrepreneurial initiative.

Another identification of entrepreneurship which fell short of a definition was made by the French economist, J.B. Say, in the early years of the nineteenth century. Consider the profit on a project, subtract the proportion of the profit which is the return on the capital and the remainder is termed entrepreneurial profit. Here again, the difficulty is in distinguishing, from each other, any of several variables.

Perhaps the most surprising aspect of the treatment of the entrepreneur in economics, to anyone with a practical orientation, is the apparent lack of any attempt until the last fifteen years to describe actual entrepreneurs and modify theory accordingly. Had this been done, there might have been earlier recognition that most activities regarded as entrepreneurial are not associated with equilibria but are essentially phenomena of disequilibrium. Opportunities arise, combinations of labour and capital are put together and the entrepreneur moves on to the next problem. For him, the whole process is fundamentally one of disequilibrium and it continues indefinitely. Equilibrium never enters into his thinking and for him it is never approached. Only if the results of what he has done in the past are examined may the concept have any relevance at all.

The entrepreneur, disequilibrium and the approach of the Austrian school

A different approach to classical economics on entrepreneurship has been taken by the Austrian School whose principal exponent has been J.A. Schumpeter. In his Theory of Economic Development (1911), the entrepreneur is portrayed as a key stimulus behind economic growth. Starting from an equilibrium position, the entrepreneur disturbs the situation and creates change until a new equilibrium is reached. For the purposes of a broad view of economic growth, such a theory may well be in agreement with practical observation. After all, from a national standpoint nearly all entrepreneurial activities are insignificantly small and may be judged only by their results or product.

What is actually happening at the entrepreneur's level may be overlooked if the concern is with the broad sweep of economic progress. Indeed, it will have to be overlooked, since the analysis will be from historic, national statistics on the productive structure. These will include the component for entrepreneurial effort and output, but it will be swamped by the activities of mature corporations reflected in the same figures.

Two more theories of entrepreneurship

Though Schumpeter's view may be less appropriate to the actual conditions of the entrepreneur, two subsequent theories have taken economics to a point where it should at least reflect practical observation. In Leibenstein's X-efficiency theory (1978), the starting point for the entrepreneur is a situation where there are vast gaps in information about the production function and a shortfall in a firm's productive potential. A creative response by the entrepreneur partially fills these gaps by a combination of knowledge, fresh ability and production factors. Full efficiency may not be reached however, as difficulties will arise such as reconciling the differing aims and objectives of individuals within the firm.

In another theory, I.M. Kirzner (1973), also stresses the inherent disequilibrium of the entrepreneur's initial position, a state characterised by mistakes, missed opportunities and previous bad decisions. The entrepreneur then perceives the opportunities and responds in a way which creates changes towards equilibrium. While there is similarity between the theories of Kirzner and Leibenstein, the detail from Kirzner's applies to what an entrepreneur is actually doing, rather than to his activity over a longer time period, taken in the context of a firm's approximation to its theoretical productive potential.

While it is not possible to predict an entrepreneur's actions from the theories, they do sharpen the definition of entrepreneurial functions to include the introduction of new organisational methods, products, processes, markets and supply sources. All of these activities initially require new information to which it is essential to be alert, a quality which most would associate with entrepreneurship. Such help with a definition is still a long way short of the substantial practical assistance which many buy-out teams might have hoped to find in economic theory as a whole.

The entrepreneur and social psychology

Some of the shortcomings of economic theory may have value in helping to understand the neglect of the entrepreneur. They have also provided a starting point for the development of the subject of entrepreneurial psychology through failing to provide adequate answers to the question of why economic growth has occurred. An early influential work in this development was Max Weber's The Protestant Ethic and the Spirit of Capitalism, originally published in German in 1904. In this, Weber noted the association between entrepreneurs, Protestantism and economic growth in eighteenth century England and concluded they were unlikely to have been motivated by money alone. After all, Protestants of the time disdained conspicuous consumption and made a virtue of frugal habits. Other motives must therefore have been operating for them in addition to money and these Weber aggregated as, 'an irrational sense of having done his job well'. Social and domestic conditions were concluded to have affected this 'irrational sense' and these were under the influence of religion.

Weber's conclusions on Protestantism depended on a selective approach to history which a subsequent writer, McClelland (1961), has shown could have been readily disproved by examples available in 1904. Since then, and particularly since 1945, further situations have arisen which rule against conclusions drawn from just one religion or race. However, the lasting value of Weber's work has been in drawing attention to the influence of groups on social conditions, breaking with economists' fixation on the money motive and profit maximising and then attributing entrepreneurs' behaviour, in part at least, to social causes. Certainly his work has been highly influential.

The two works with perhaps the best claim to founding the subject of entrepreneurial psychology were both written at roughly the same time, both were intended primarily to explain problems of economic growth and both appear to have been influenced strongly by Weber and Schumpeter. The first to be published was D.C. McClelland's The Achieving Society (1961). While working on psychological tests in the 1950s to investigate leadership, as R.J.B. Bruce (1976) has outlined, McClelland had isolated a quality in subjects which amounted to a general concern to get ahead in the world. This he termed, a 'need for achievement', an identity abbreviated to *n* Achievement or *n* Ach.

High *n* Achievement in men in the US was found more often among the middle, rather than upper or lower classes and was found to be influenced by social and domestic backgrounds. A variety of characteristics were consequent upon high *n* Achievement. Those with high *n* Achievement are more resistant to social pressures, choose experts rather than friends as working partners, are more active in community

activities, tend to volunteer more readily for psychological experiments, dislike repetitive routine work,
and need to know the results of their decisions. If
taking a risk, they will choose a moderate risk which
they can then work to reduce, rather than either a high
risk with an outside chance of high return, or a low risk
with little challenge. Despite the overt effects of high *n*
Achievement, those with it cannot give an account of
what their inner concern for achievement is motivated
by.

With all these properties, *n* Achievement was
equated by McClelland with Weber's 'irrational sense'
and then advanced in a similar manner to Schumpeter's entrepreneur as a major agent of national
economic growth. It would not necessarily be the only
factor behind growth, but it would have a central role
to play. Societies would build up *n* Achievement,
produce more entrepreneurs and these in turn would
promote faster growth. The indices of achievement
from various times through history, produced by
McClelland, are sufficient to relate *n* Achievement to
the phenomenon of economic growth and to imply a
connection with entrepreneurship, though with some
doubt over its exact role. In particular, McClelland's
central thesis of *n* Achievement providing a means for
the prediction of current national economic growth,
let alone for its providing a principle to explain
international comparisons of current growth, has met
with a most unfavourable response, Baumol (1968).

The second work which founded the subject was
E.E. Hagen's *On the Theory of Social Change: How
Economic Growth Begins* (1962), of which a summarised version appears in Hagen (1963). From extensive earlier investigations into the religious, ethnic and
social backgrounds of entrepreneurs at various times
in several countries, Hagen had stressed the importance of minority groups in supplying leadership at
times of growth and change. Building on his earlier

work, Hagen now attempted to derive a cause for historic growth from several economic histories, but notably Japan and eighteenth century England. With entrepreneurship strongly orientated around minority groups with any or all of social, cultural, religious and ethnic qualities in his examples, Hagen isolates a couple of events which precede the emergence of entrepreneurs.

Starting with traditional society in which there is rigid social structure, little prospect of social change and low economic growth, but some attraction in the status quo for those with values and advantage, change is seen as starting with the withdrawal of status respect for a class or group. An initial reaction of anger gives way to the gradual loss of role values which is cumulative and may be spread over several generations until they have largely or entirely gone. Hagen terms this situation 'normlessness'. Other writers have used the terms, 'shiftlessness' and 'retreatism' for broadly the same condition. From this state, individuals emerge who are alienated from traditional values, who are driven by a desire to prove themselves and who are creative. Hagen termed these characteristics 'creativity'. The entrepreneurs are formed from those with high creativity and among their attributes is a strong drive to be independent.

Though derived in very different ways from the psychological tests which gave rise to *n* Achievement, the concept of creativity is very similar. Creativity refers to a group as opposed to individuals, it applies over a long period of time and above all, it stresses independence, but in the end it covers qualities and abilities which for the most part are identical with *n* Achievement. Nonetheless, through being derived by a different approach, it has raised different questions and inspired a different train of subsequent research.

Some points of definition

A problem with work which followed McClelland and Hagen has been confusion over definitions and in particular, those of managers and entrepreneurs. As M.F.R. Kets de Vries (1977) has indicated, the problem has recurred and indeed, it continues to this day. That it arose in the first place may be related to the broad functions attributed to entrepreneurs by the early writers. Thus an early study of a large sample of entrepreneurs in the US by O.F. Collins, D.G. Moore and D.B. Unwalla (1964) found no overall association between *n* Achievement and entrepreneurs. However as Bruce (1976) has demonstrated, the point hinges entirely on definition, since the sample taken failed to distinguish between entrepreneurs who start small businesses which remain small, the vast majority in fact, and those who succeed in establishing an expanding business. That the sample included some of the latter, Bruce (1976) determines from the results of the section of the study investigating risk-taking and gambling. The gambler is prepared to operate a system at which eventual loss is inevitable. He is low in *n* Achievement. Those who take calculated risks and work towards winning are high in *n* Achievement. There were some high achievers in the sample.

Another entrepreneurial characteristic immediately apparent from a practical study by O.F. Collins and others (1964), was independence. Entrepreneurs were seen as men with a quality described as diffuse restlessness: men who travel light, fast and alone, never resting content with past success. This independence had not even been identified by McClelland, whose definition of an entrepreneur had emphasised decision-making responsibilities. Consequently, he had not come to distinguish between those who break away from corporations and those who remain. Hagen had covered the point, but had not given it the same stress.

The dilemma for the definition of the entrepreneur based solely on functions generally associated with entrepreneurship such as risk-taking, decision-making, strategy formulation and so on, is that these functions are also carried out in greater or lesser degree by people in corporations whose careers have involved advancement relative to a bureaucracy. However while any definition of entrepreneurship must accommodate this point there are nevertheless certain functions which imply a tendency towards bureaucracy or towards independent control, which are more readily associated with corporate management and entrepreneurship respectively. In this context, the definitions suggested by M.J.K. Stanworth and J. Curran (1973) seem particularly apt.

Management is defined as an activity which centres on the maintenance and extension of existing business enterprise. The manager has a well-defined role and a career path.

Entrepreneurship is defined as creating a set of social relations where none existed before in an unstructured, high-risk environment.

These definitions are insufficient on their own to resolve all the confusion in the literature, but then with a requirement to accommodate both independence and a distinction between those who stay small and others who achieve something more, it is to be doubted whether a single definition ever could. Rather, the confusion is overcome by superimposing on these definitions the classification suggested by Bruce (1976).

In Bruce's classification, there is full recognition that many entrepreneurs with high achievement motivation are to be found within corporations. These are termed modal entrepreneurs, a name adopted from T.C. Cochran (1965), who viewed those at the top of corporations as being in a modal position relative to the confluence of social forces at its apex, deflecting and influencing some of them, but having never broken away from them. A modal entrepreneur is motivated to get ahead in an organisation, but serves it because that is what he is paid to do.

An altogether different motivation is shown by those who break clear from the protection of a corporation. These, the independent entrepreneurs, are running their companies because that is what they choose to do. Control will be through a shareholding and the motive for independence was to obtain that control and build up an organisation. The aim in obtaining control for the vast majority, who succeed in running a small business, is not to be controlled by others. These Bruce terms ubiquitous. On the other hand, those with high *n* Achievement who succeed in building a major organisation, Bruce terms élite. The resulting classification is simple:

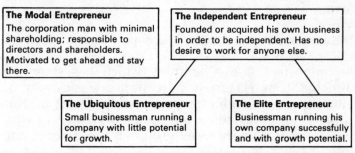

The Modal Entrepreneur
The corporation man with minimal shareholding; responsible to directors and shareholders. Motivated to get ahead and stay there.

The Independent Entrepreneur
Founded or acquired his own business in order to be independent. Has no desire to work for anyone else.

The Ubiquitous Entrepreneur
Small businessman running a company with little potential for growth.

The Elite Entrepreneur
Businessman running his own company successfully and with growth potential.

Source: R.J.B. Bruce (1976)

The questions raised by this classification and the two preceding definitions greatly simplify the assessment of entrepreneurship and assist a review of the literature on the subject. To what extent is a function managerial or entrepreneurial? Is it being carried out within a corporation or outside it? Will it lead to growth and substantial organisation or not? The answers to these and similar questions resolve most of the confusion.

Development of the subject of entrepreneurship and entrepreneurial psychology

Several themes have been developed and verified by research since the subject was opened up and some of these will now be examined. Much of the subject matter is open to the criticisms which can be levelled at social investigation in general; imprecise results, the need for numerous subjective assessments by either the reader, or the researcher, or both and the use of small, selected samples in certain instances. With such a background it is inappropriate to consider whether the axioms of entrepreneurial psychology are right or wrong. Rather, it is important to appreciate how and why the ideas were investigated and which of them may now be considered to have withstood the test of time.

Entrepreneurship and minority groups

An important line of enquiry which has stemmed directly from Hagen has been the association of minority groups with entrepreneurship. There are two approaches: find some entrepreneurs and see who has come from a minority group and vice versa, the former being the easier method. Several writers have confirmed or remarked on the relationship; among others, O.F. Collins and others (1964), Bruce (1976), J. Ronen (1983). They have described the very high incidence of entrepreneurs to be found among immigrants into the US, into several Latin American countries and also among the Santri Moslems of Java, the Jains, Parsees and Sikhs of India, the Indian and Chinese communities of South East Asia, the Lebanese in North Africa, the Ibos in Nigeria and the Jews in a variety of places. Together with the historical examples of Protestants in England and France and the Samurai in Japan, these groups are sufficiently diverse to suggest that the phenomenon of entrepreneurship is not specific to race or religion but relies on individual and social qualities which arise from minority status in large measure. Their diversity and typical status also suggest general support for Hagen's thesis of group role deterioration and social marginality preceding the generation of entrepreneurs.

The motivation for growth: achievement or power?

An early difficulty in applying McClelland's concept of *n* Achievement was that it may or may not cover a large range of motives, aims and abilities; that it was too general for specific applications. McClelland went some way towards meeting the difficulty by distinguishing two other motives from *n* Achievement. These were *n* Affiliation and *n* Power. The issue might have been resolved from this distinction had there not been severe limitations to the methods for measuring *n* Achievement.

The approach used by McClelland, involving perception tests, might be acceptable when used for research in an academic environment with known administrators, but they are open to abuse and error when commercial pressures are introduced. Possibly for this reason there has been a lack of research into *n* Achievement possessed by those who actually decide to own and manage a business. Indeed as Ronen (1983) has pointed out, there has been no known research to date to relate the decision to n Achievement. Partly as a result, rival theories have emerged which attribute the drive to build a large organisation to the desire for power. These are perhaps less convincing than McClelland's work since other researchers have found that the power motive tends to have a perverse effect on the running of a business by impairing the perception of markets and of people, so leading to poor delegation and inefficient organisational structure. Nonetheless, at the time of writing the nature of the roles of power and achievement motivation for the entrepreneur must remain an open question.

Independence, role-deterioration and social marginality: the emergence of the determining event

Hagen's cycle of the loss of traditional values had referred to a group over a long time period and this might have had little relevance for the analysis of an individual entrepreneur. Attention had been drawn by him however to the concepts of role deterioration and social marginality and practical research related these to actual entrepreneurs, O.F. Collins and others (1964). Subsequent work has confirmed the relationship: Stanworth and Curran (1973), Kets de Vries (1977), and Bruce (1976). Once social marginality had been recognised, the implications from the extensive work on the subject elsewhere could be invoked and searched for. The psychological picture presented of an individual with a disturbed background against which he is attempting to react is at times unsettling, even alarming and as Bruce (1976) has indicated, may equally well refer to a criminal, hobo or pop star. Bruce postulates that social marginality is consequent upon role deterioration which in turn was caused by some determining event. This is most likely to have been experienced in late childhood, adolescence or early adulthood and can take any of a variety of forms. Of crucial importance is how it was perceived and reacted to by the subject. Founding a business may be seen as an attempt to resolve the conflicts arising from social marginality, a resolution which is unlikely to be successful for the individual even if the business is a success.

Immediately it may be objected that while such a background may be attributed to many entrepreneurs, there are exceptions. Stanworth and Curran (1973) distinguish between first and second generation entrepreneurs, many of the latter not exhibiting social marginality. Developing the view, Bruce (1976) advances the idea that all independent first generation entrepreneurs have experienced role-deterioration, though this may be further than many may care to extend the principle, while accepting a lower incidence of it among second and third generation entrepreneurs. A problem of practical investigation on this point is that the patterns of motives and backgrounds may be sufficiently complex in reality as to limit the application of such broad conclusions. A review of much recent work in Scotland by T. Milne and J. Lewis (1982), covers several unpublished papers which, while confirming many of the concepts in this appendix, also indicate the moderating influence of detail. Actual practical detail can outweigh a concept such as social marginality and indeed has been found to do so by D.R. Sellyn (1980). In a community he studied in which two thirds of the economically active population were self-employed, he has suggested that the exceptions were those who took up employment.

Management development and succession problems

The problem of succession in small companies has long been recognised. R.C. Christensen (1953) noted that the issue is frequently ignored, possibly because it becomes identified with loss or losing out. A variety of factors may be operating on management development and some of the issues and dangers for the growing organisation are outlined by L.L. Steinmetz (1969) in his isolation of critical points in a firm's development at which the entrepreneur either has to relax his hold and develop the management structure, or risk disaster. In this, the entrepreneur is likely to be his worst enemy if the qualities outlined by Kets de Vries (1977) are remotely correct. The preference for patriarchal relationships, high degree of anxiety, uncomfortable relationships with authority figures and general refusal to delegate, all contribute towards a structure which is dominated by and dependent upon the entrepreneur. With poorly-defined tasks, much role conflict and tension, the more capable subordinates tend to leave and so contribute towards a situation where external intervention to remove the entrepreneur is the only option for succession. Thus many of the qualities which led the entrepreneur to independence in the first instance can contribute towards his downfall.

The money motive

There has been continuing interest in the motivational properties of money since Weber (1904). Perhaps the most revealing investigation was from McClelland (1961) who found that money was a minor influence for those with high *n* Achievement. The attraction of money for its own sake on the other hand, was to be found among those with low *n* Achievement, the members of corporations who never get near the top, the small businessmen who stay small. The finding has been confirmed by D. Watkins (1973) and J-C. Ettinger (1983), though Ronen (1983) refers to the slightly different motive of avoiding future poverty. Money may be an attraction too, where it forms an index of achievement, McClelland (1961).

Job creation as a motive

With entrepreneurs widely seen as agents for promoting economic growth and inter alia, reducing unemployment, Ettinger (1983) investigated whether job creation is part of entrepreneurial motivation in

Belgium. It was found to play no part at all, a result which is fully in line with the theory of social marginality.

Association with small businesses and other entrepreneurs

The connection between second generation entrepreneurs and a much lower incidence of social marginality has already been referred to. What really does appear to be a catalyst for entrepreneurial activity is some connection with other entrepreneurs and with small businesses in general. J. Deeks (1972) found that a majority have some connection of this nature while A.C. Cooper (1971) found that the incidence of entrepreneurial generation was higher by a factor of eight in firms with less than 500 employees.

The entrepreneur and management buy-outs

In view of these results, it may be questioned whether there are people with entrepreneurial potential who prior to management buy-outs, would not have developed it. Stanworth and Curran (1973) refer to studies which indicated that of those who wanted to run a business, only a small proportion actually succeed in breaking away from their current organisation. This certainly indicates a reserve of demand and enthusiasm and, cautiously too, a reserve of ability.

A second question is whether it is possible to cross the divide from corporation to independence without suffering all the disadvantages traditionally associated with entrepreneurship. The answer here is almost certain to provide the key to whether management buy-outs have created a new style of entrepreneur, with significantly different characteristics to those exhibited by a majority of independent entrepreneurs hitherto. A preliminary answer appears to be that there is little difference. Those who were destined to become modal entrepreneurs can carry out essentially the same function from the different, though comparable, position provided by many buy-outs. However the implication follows of preserving many aspects of the former organisation to ensure an orderly transition to independence. With continuous support from an organisation, these new independent entrepreneurs need never face the exposure or require the self-reliance of either the ubiquitous entrepreneur, or the future elite entrepreneur at the time of a conventional start-up.

Bibliography

Aaronovitch, S., and Sawyer, M.C., *Big Business,* Macmillan, 1975.

Baumol, W.J., 'Entrepreneurship in Economic History', *American Economic Review,* No 58, 1968.

Blackstone, L., and Franks, D., *Management Buy-Outs,* 1984 edition. Special Report No. 164, The Economist Intelligence Unit. London 1984.

Boddewyn, J.J., *International Divestment,* Business International, 1976.

Bruce, R.J.B., *The Entrepreneurs,* Libertarian Books, Bedford, 1976.

Business Graduates Association, *The Successful Spin-Off,* London, 1980.

Casson, M., *The Entrepreneur,* Martin Robertson, Oxford, 1982.

Christensen, C.R., *Management Succession in Small and Growing Enterprises,* Harvard University Press, Boston, 1953.

Cochran, T.C., 'The Entrepreneur in Economic Change; Explorations In Enterpreneurial History'. Reprinted in: Kilby, P. (ed.), *Enterpreneurship and Economic Development,* Free Press, 1971.

Collins, O.F., Moore, D.G., and Unwalla, D.B., *The Enterprising Man,* Michigan State University Business Studies, 1964.

Cooper, A.C., 'Spin-Offs and Technical Entrepreneurship', *IEEE Trans. on Engineering Management,* Vol. EM-18, No. 1, Feb., 1971.

Deeks, J., 'The Educational and Occupational History of Owner Managers and Management', *Journal of Management Studies,* May, 1972.

Ettinger, J-C., 'Some Belgian Evidence on Entrepreneurial Personality', *European Small Business Journal,* Winter 1983.

Gargiulo, A.F. and Levine, S.J., *The Leveraged Buy-Out,* American Management Association, 1982.

Gorb, P., 'The Demerger Bandwagon Hits Trail', *Accountancy Age,* 4 April 1980.

Hagen, E.E., *On the Theory of Social Change: How Economic Growth Begins,* Dorsey Press, Homewood, Illinois, 1962, and Tavistock Publications, 1964.

Hagen, E.E., 'How Economic Growth Begins: a Theory of Social Change', Reprinted in: Kilby, P. (ed.), *Entrepreneurship and Economic Development,* Free Press, 1971.

Haggett, D.S., 'Negotiating the Deal', Proceedings of a National Conference on Management Buy-Outs, University of Nottingham, 1981.

Hannah, L., and Kay, J.A., *Concentration in Modern Industry,*Macmillan, 1977.

Hardman, J.P. and Young, M.R., 'Management Buy-outs', *Accountants Digest,* No 133, 1983.

Hayek, F.A. von, *The Road to Serfdom,* Routledge, 1944.

Hébert, R.F., and Link, A.N., *The Entrepreneur*, Praeger, 1982.

Jewkes, J., *Ordeal by Planning*, Macmillan, 1947.

Johnson, Sir A., *The City Take-over Code*, Oxford University Press, 1980.

M.F.R. Kets de Vries, 'The Entrepreneurial Personality', *Journal of Management Studies*, Vol. 14, No. 1, 1977.

Kirzner, I.M., *Competition and Entrepreneurship*, University of Chicago Press, 1973.

Leibenstein, H., 'Entrepreneurship and Development', *American Economic Review*, No 58, 1968.

Leibenstein, H., *General X-Efficiency Theory and Economic Development*, Oxford University Press, New York, 1978.

McClelland, D.C., *The Achieving Society*, Van Nostrand, 1961.

Michaels, D., 'A Sale Versus a Buy-out – the Management Dilemma', *Financial Times Supplement on Mergers and Acquisitions*, Autumn 1983.

Mills, A. and Miles, P., *The Buy-Out Experience*, Spicer and Pegler, 1984.

Milne, T. and Lewis, J., 'The Scottish Contribution to Entrepreneurial Studies', in Lewis, J., Stanworth, J., and Gibb., A. (eds.), *Success and Failure in Small Business*, Gower, 1984.

Peat, Marwick, Mitchell and Co., 'Management Buy-Outs and Incentive Financing', *Daily Telegraph* publication, 1982.

Ridmar Marketing Research, 'Survey of Buy-Outs', *Chief Executive*, December 1982.

Ronen, J., 'Some Insights into the Entrepreneurial Process', in Ronen, J. (ed.), *Entrepreneurship*, D.C. Heath and Co., Lexington, Massachusetts, 1983.

Schumpeter, J.A., *The Theory of Economic Development*, Harvard, 1934. (First published in German, 1911.)

Sellyn, D.R., *Jewish Businessmen in Glasgow: Patterns of Self-Employment*, unpublished MBA Dissertation, Glasgow, 1980. Quoted in Milne, T., and Lewis, J., see above.

Smith, R., 'Management Buy-Outs: Opportunities and Strategies', Proceedings of a National Conference on Management Buy-Outs, University of Nottingham, 1981.

Solow, R.M., 'Technical Change and the Aggregate Production Function', *Review of Economics and Statistics*, 1957.

Spicer and Pegler, *The Management Buy-Out*, Second ed., Spicer and Pegler, 1984.

Stanworth, M.J.K., and Curran, J., *Management Motivation in the Smaller Business*, Gower, 1973.

Steinmetz, L.L., 'Criticial Stages of Small Business Growth', *Business Horizons*, February 1969.

Watkins, D.S., 'Technical Entrepreneurship: a CIS-Atlantic View', *R and D Management*, Vol. 3, No. 2, 1973.

Weber, M., *The Protestant Ethic and the Spirit of Capitalism*, Allen and Unwin, 1930. (First published in German, 1904.)

Weinberg, M.A., Blank, M.V., and Greystoke, A.L., *Takeovers and Mergers*, 4th ed., Sweet and Maxwell, London, 1979.

Wright, D.M. and Coyne, J., 'Survey of Buy-Outs', *Sunday Times*, 9 October 1983.

Index